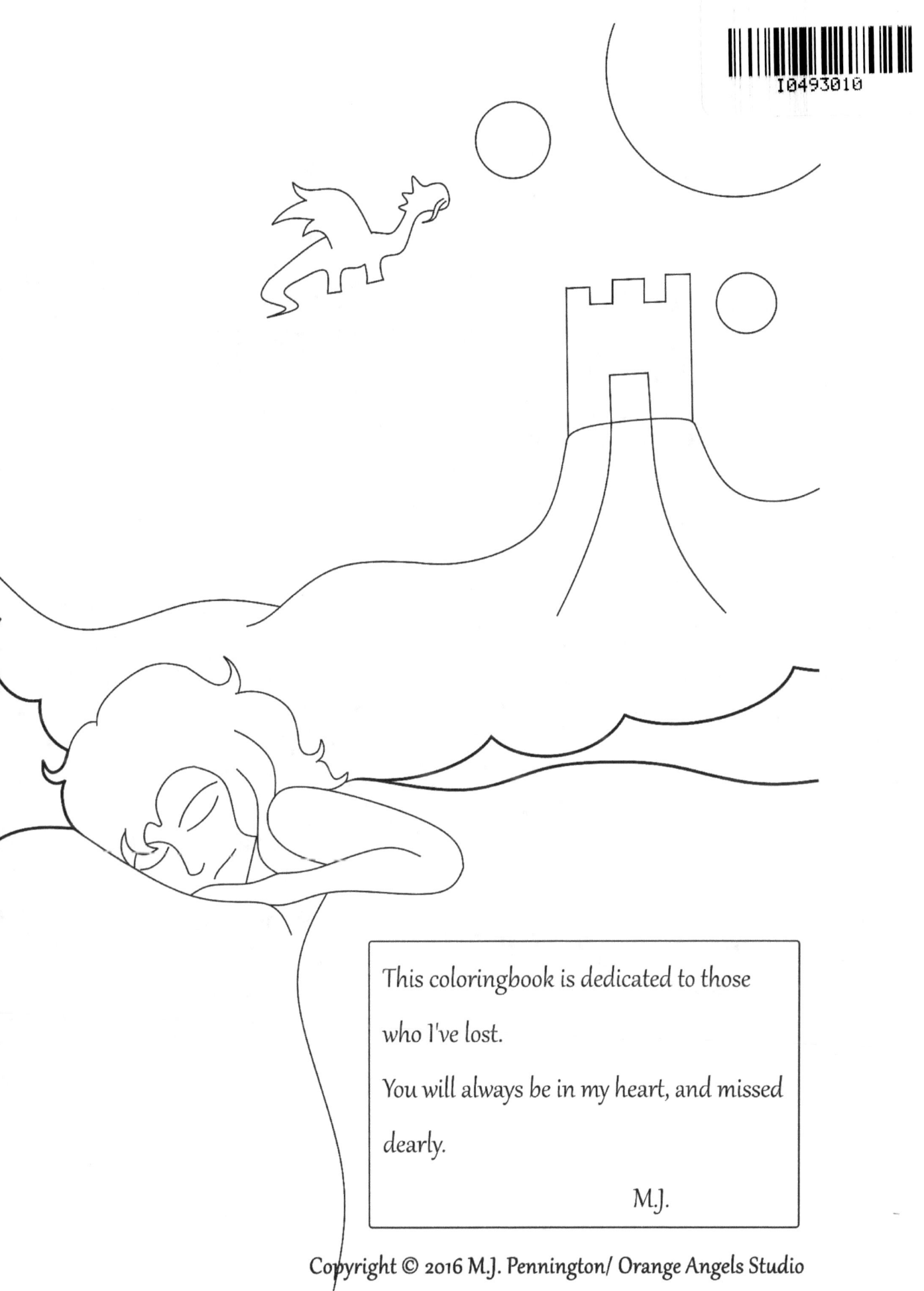

This coloringbook is dedicated to those who I've lost.

You will always be in my heart, and missed dearly.

M.J.

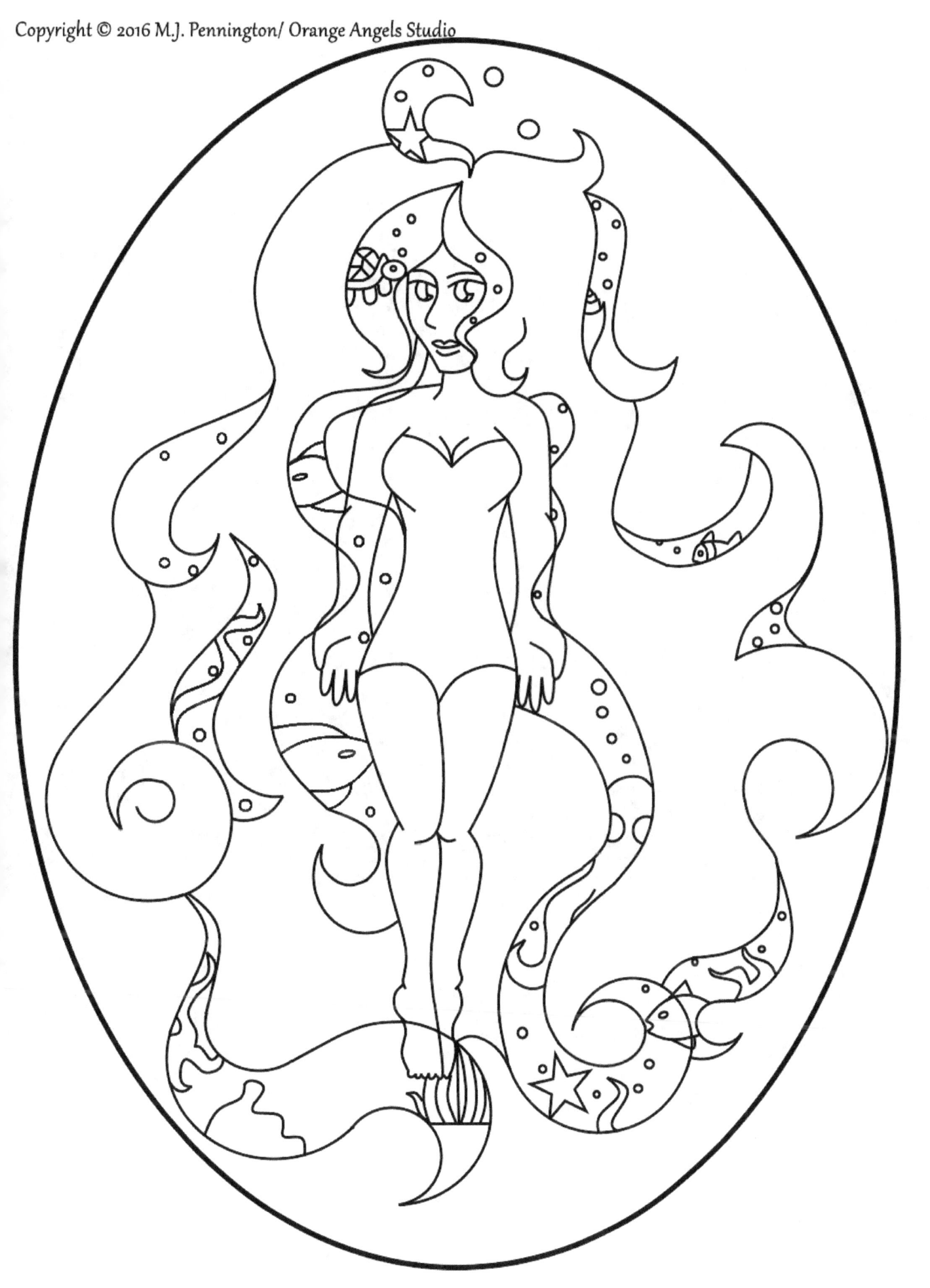

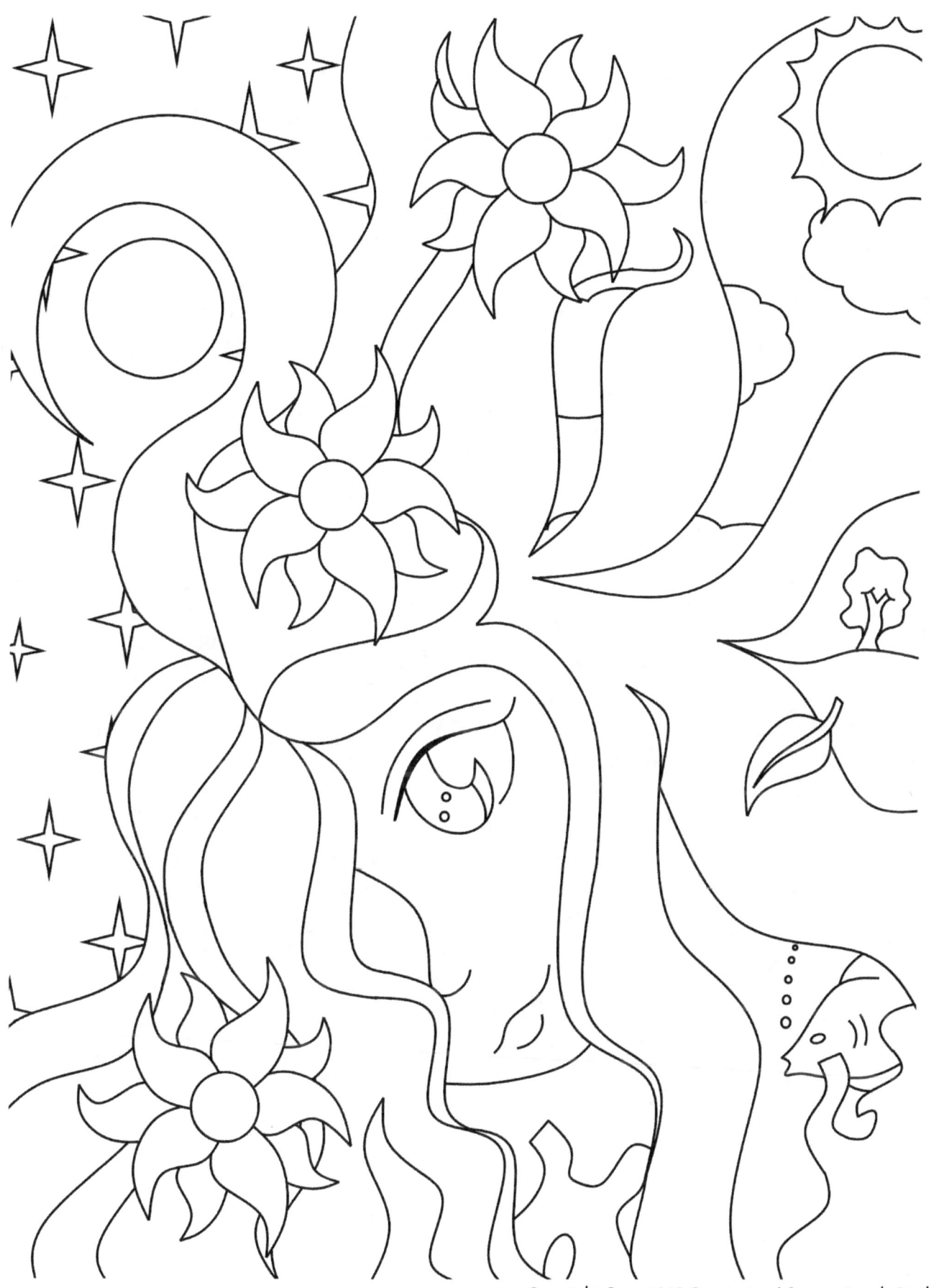

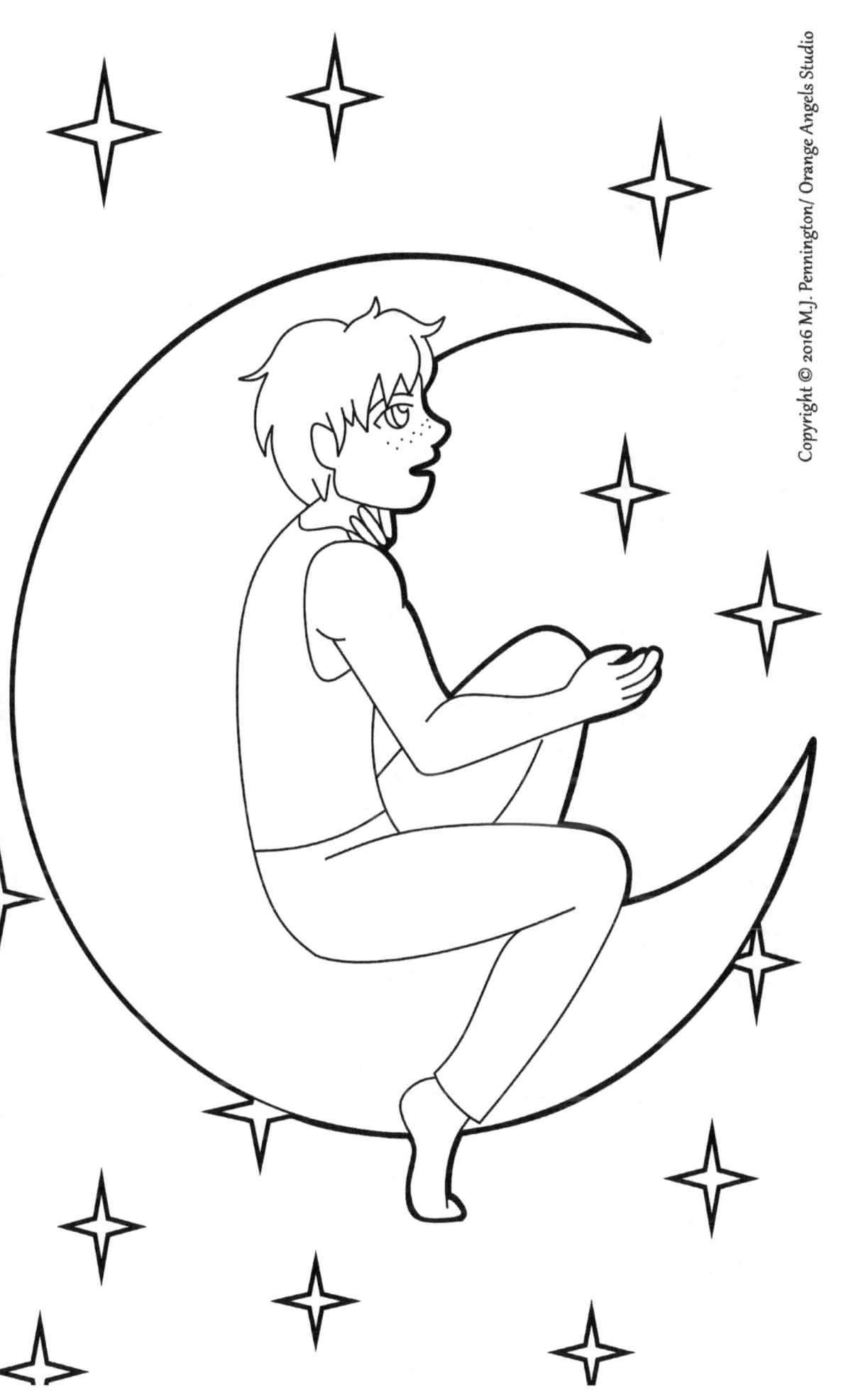

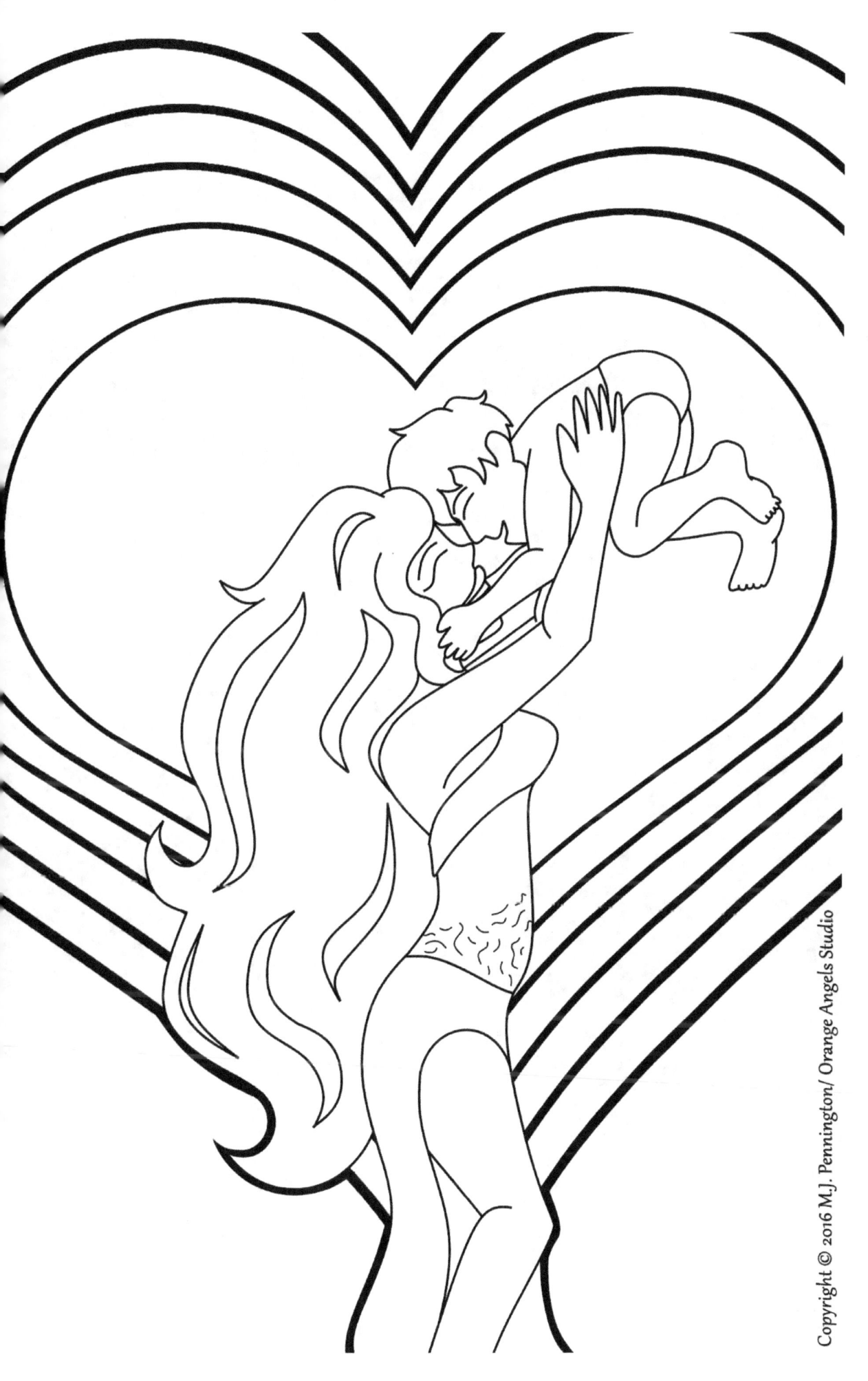

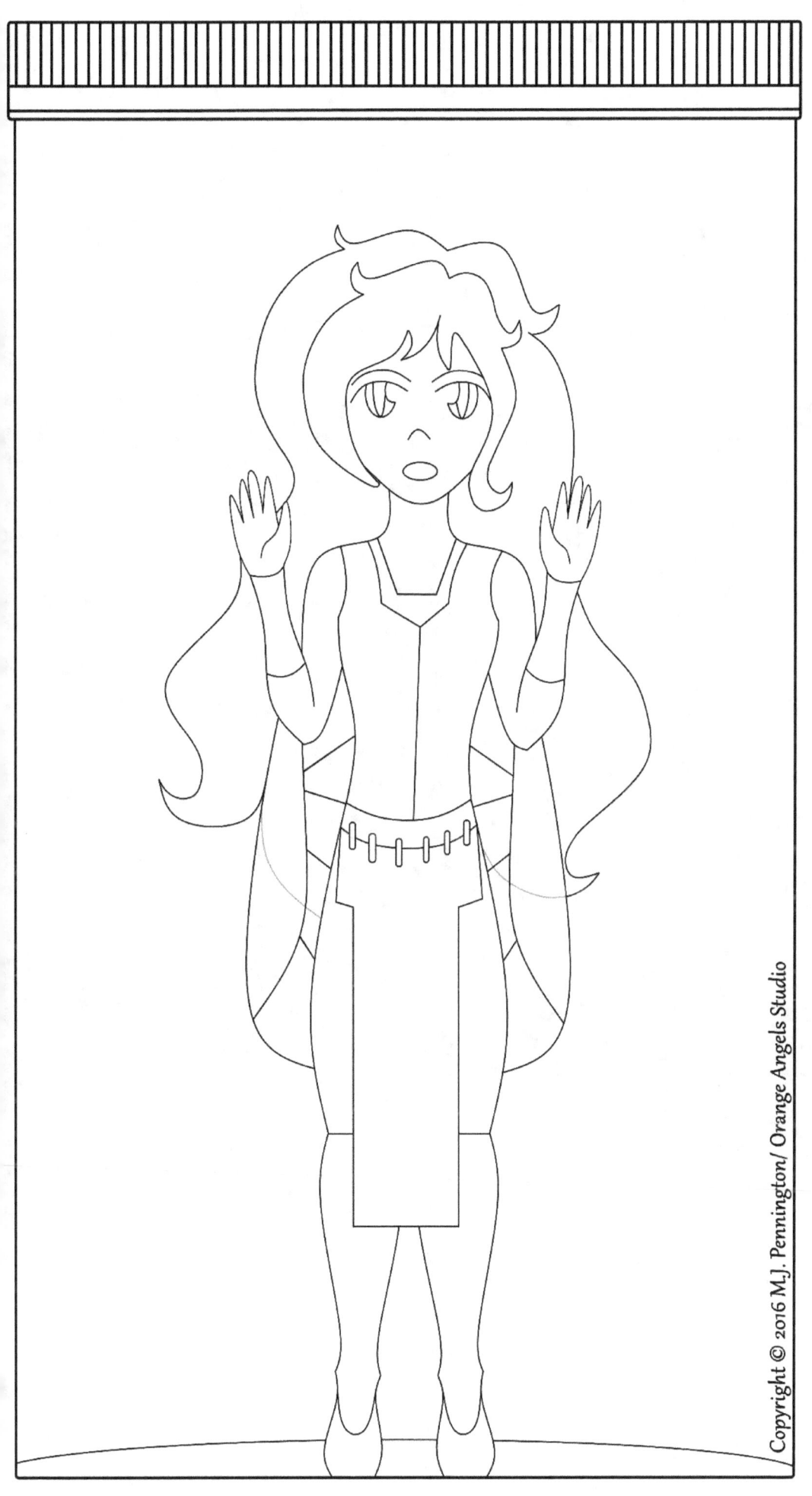

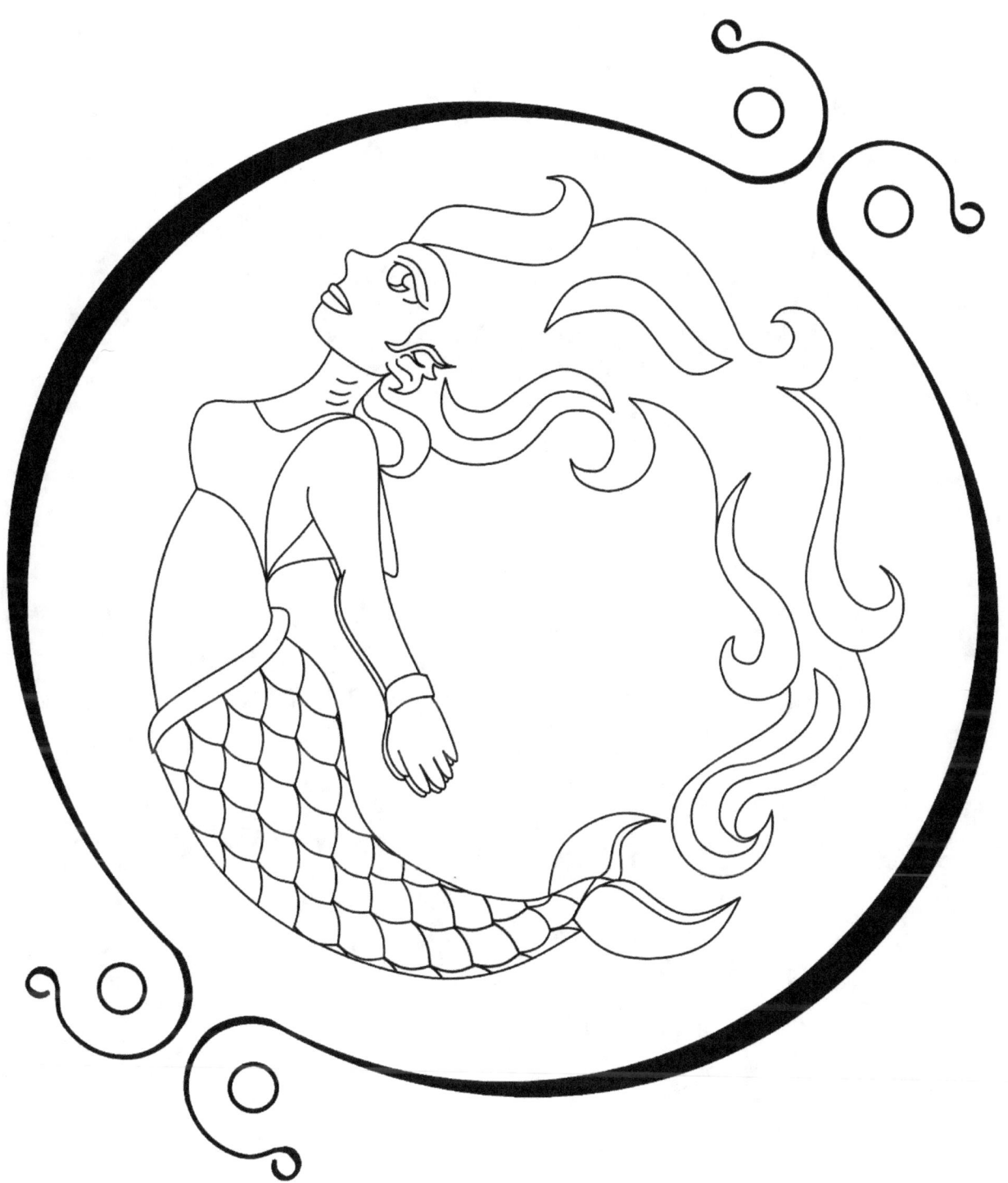

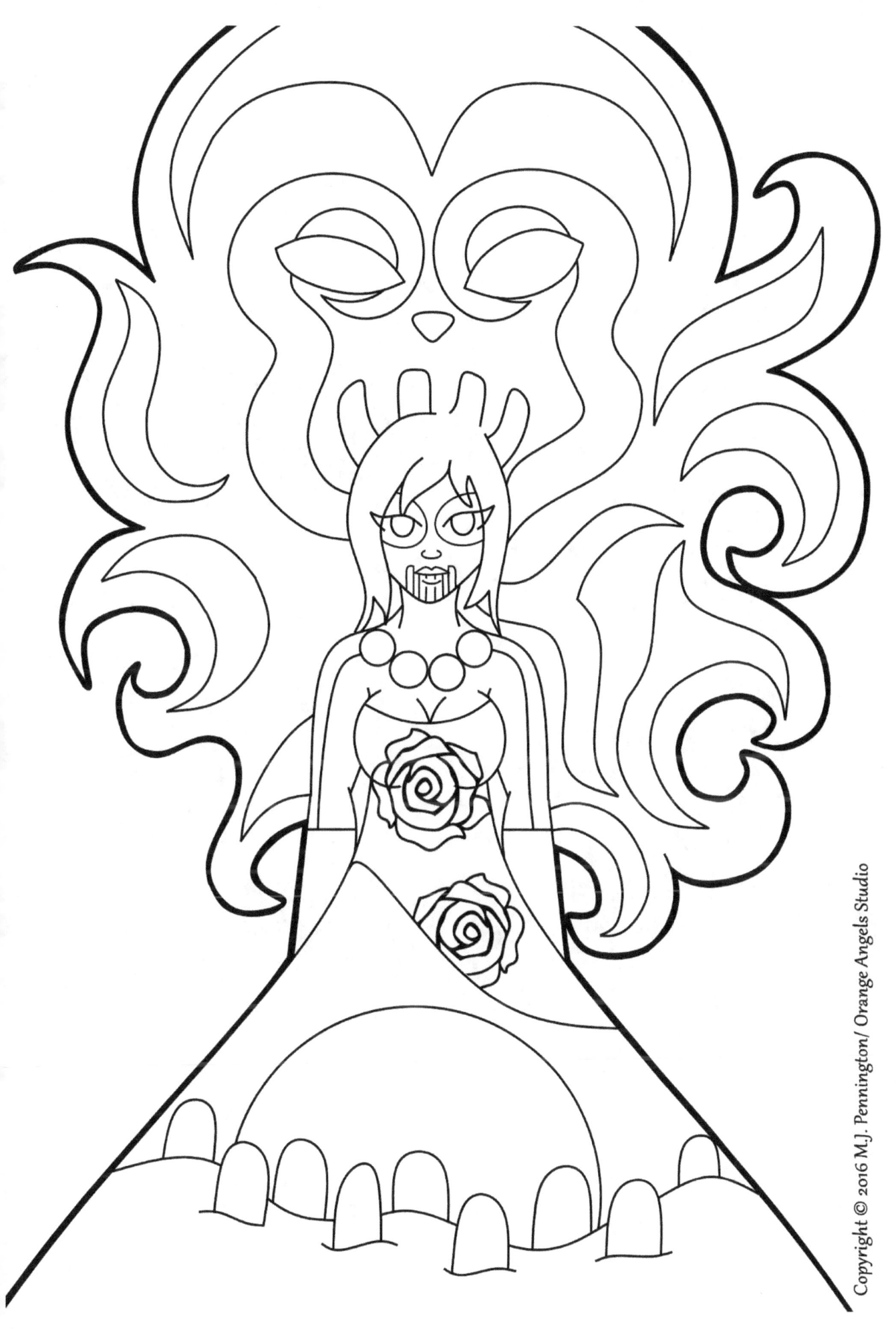

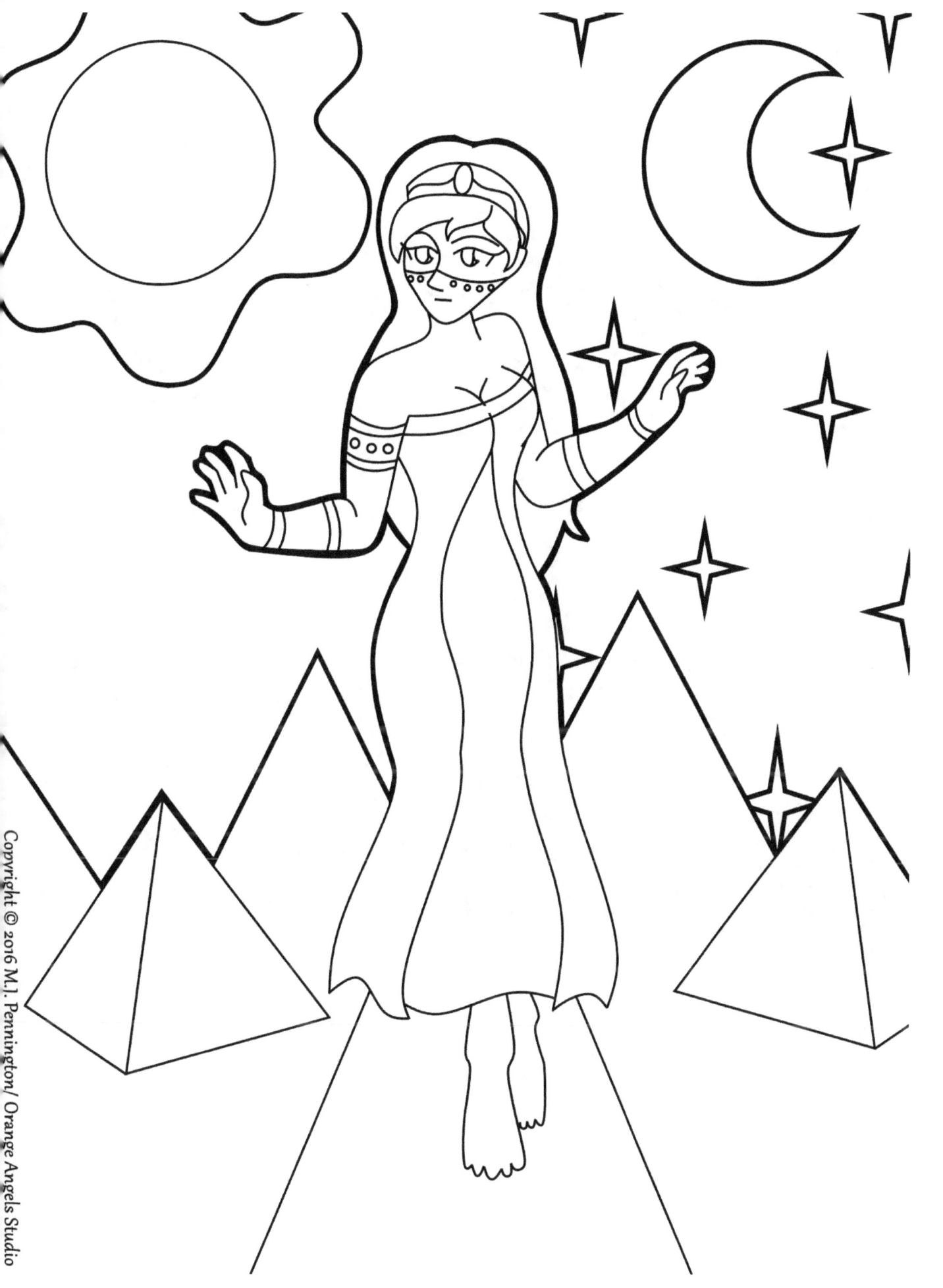

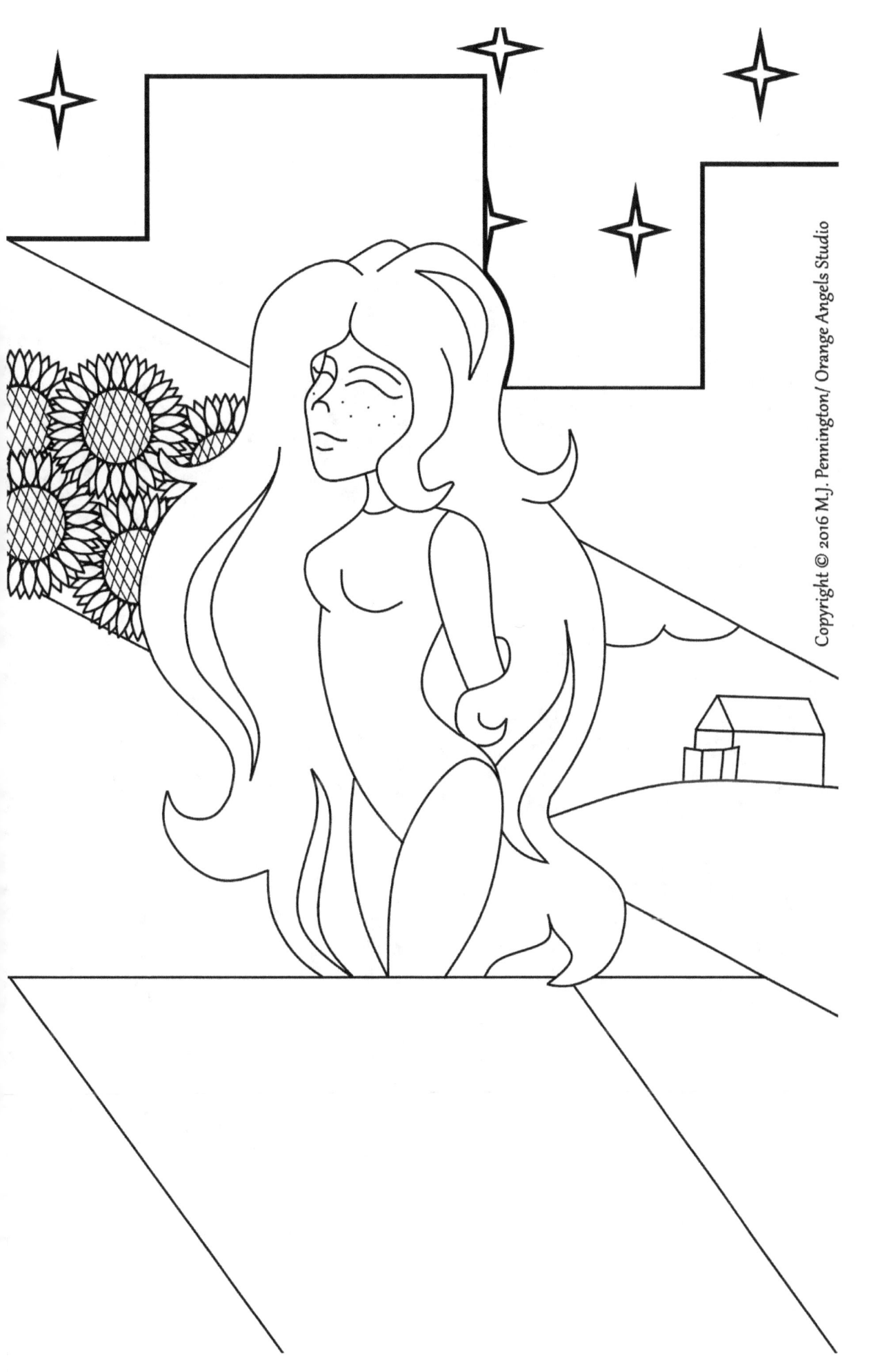

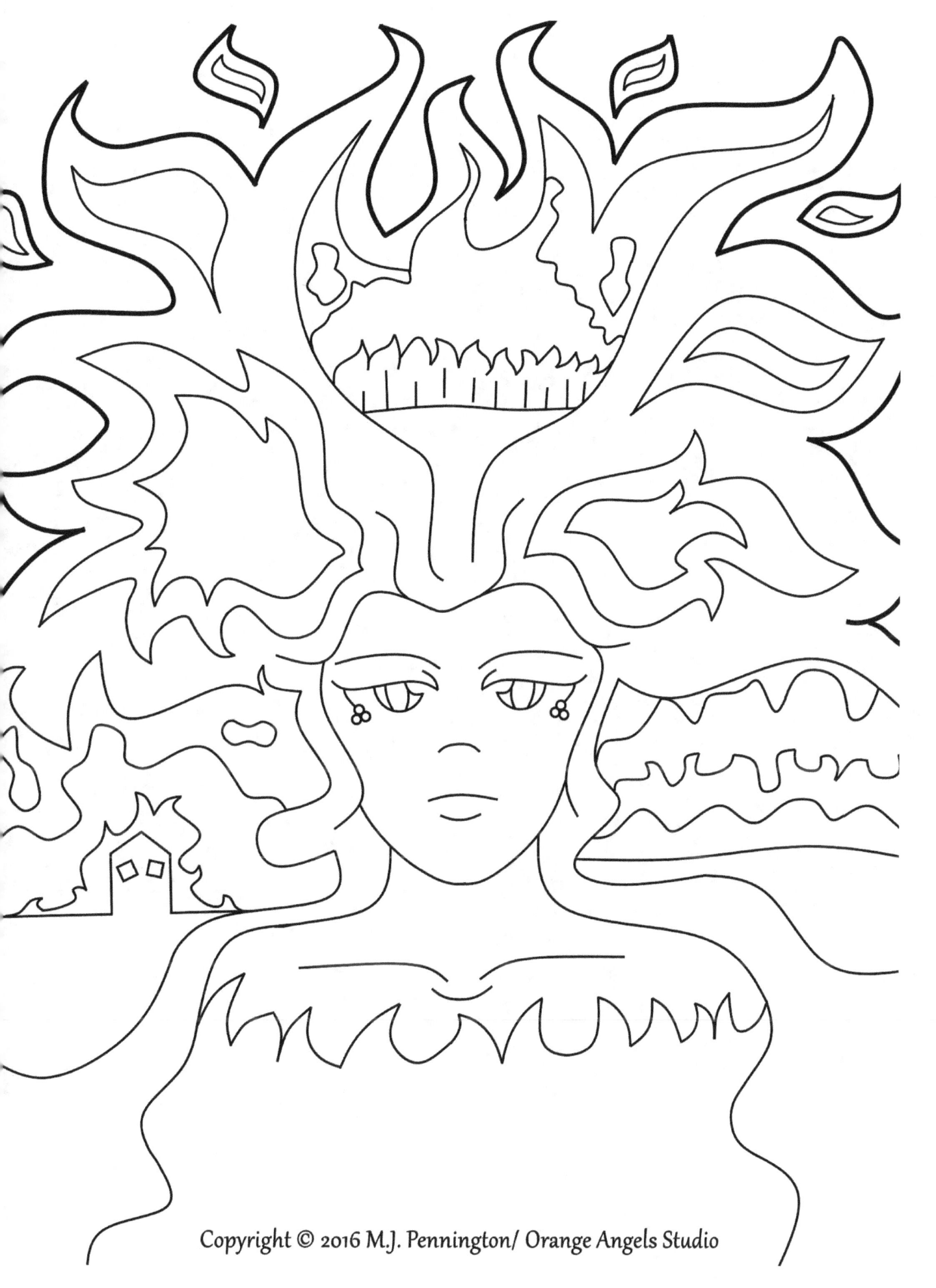

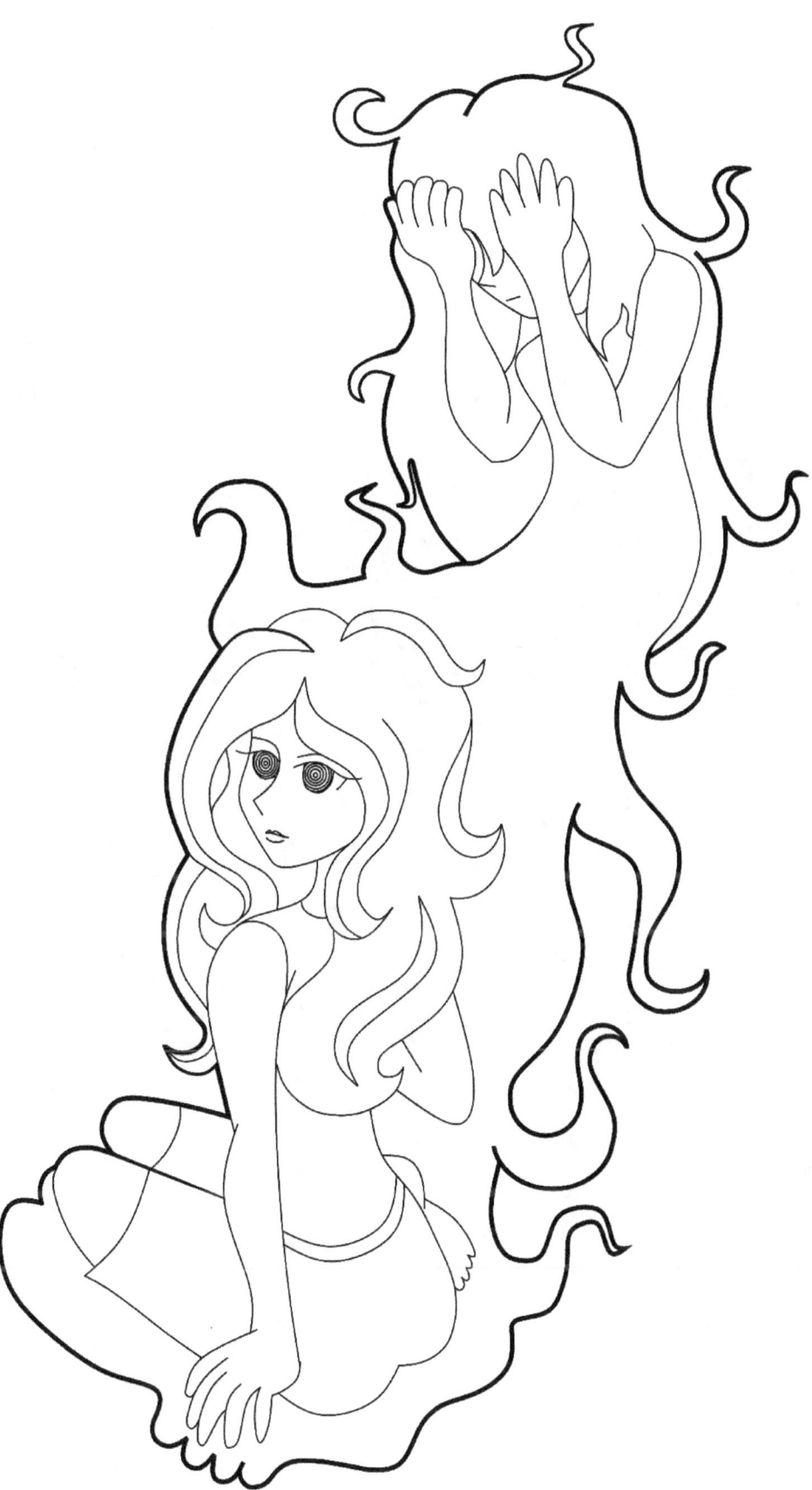

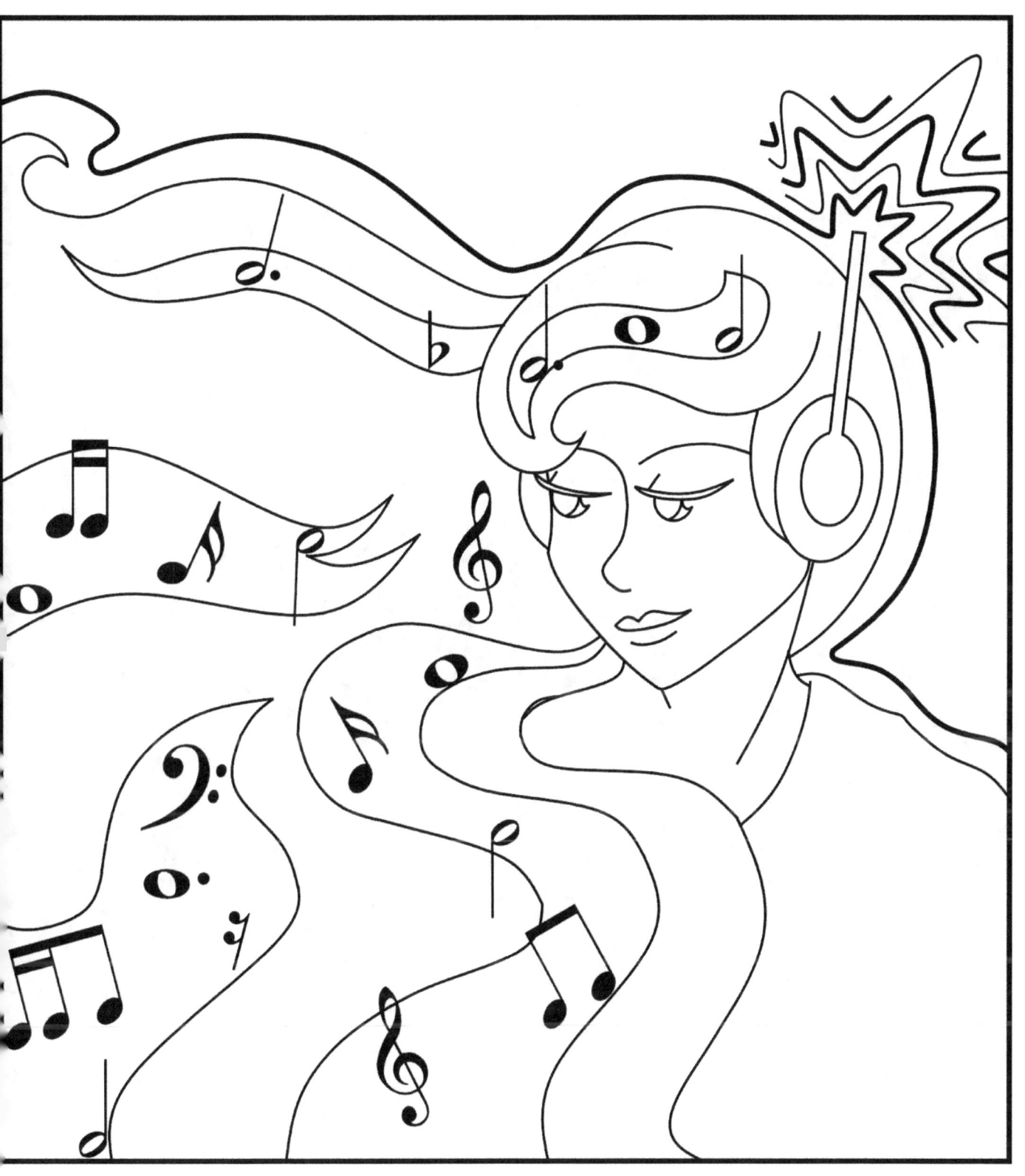

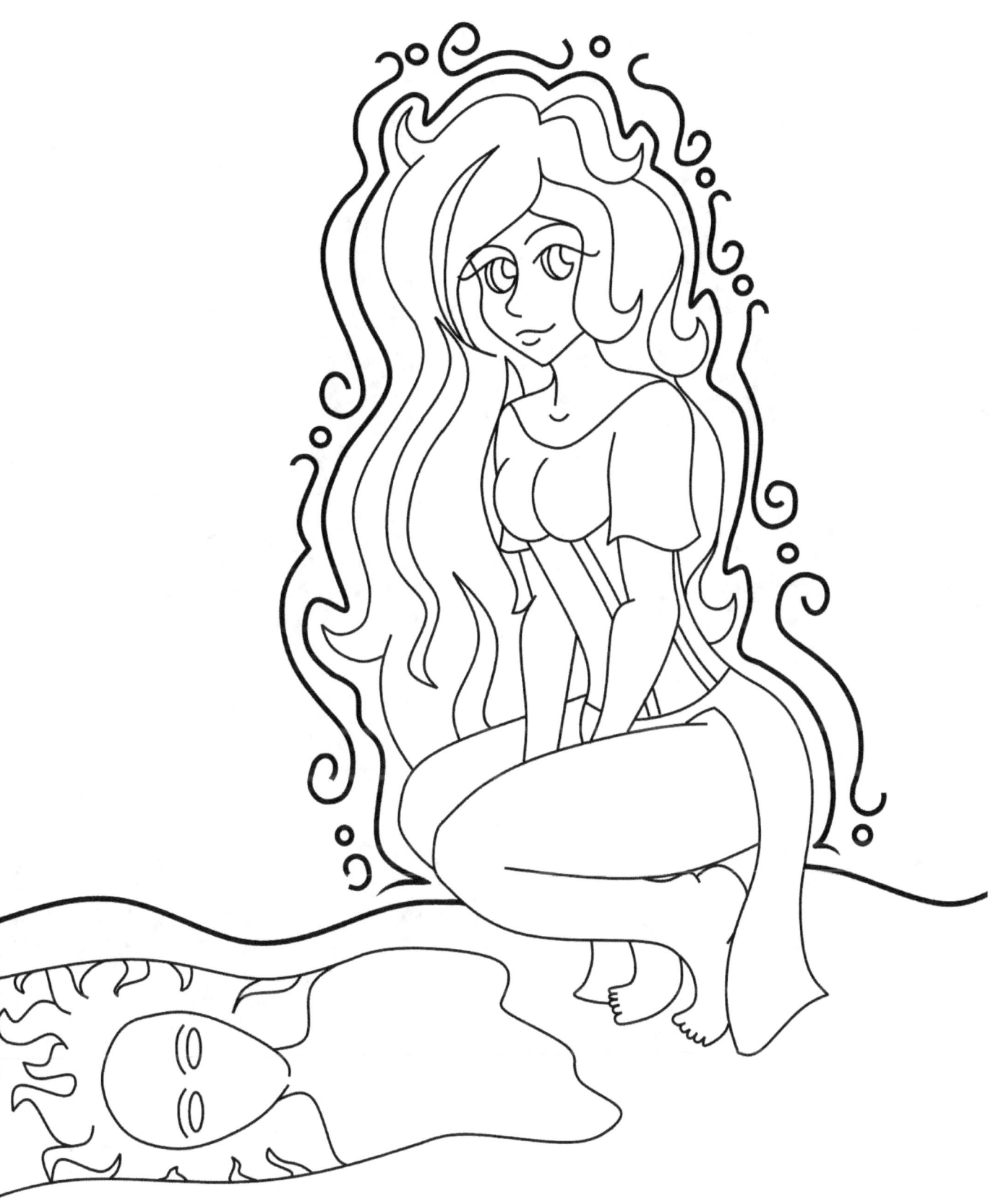

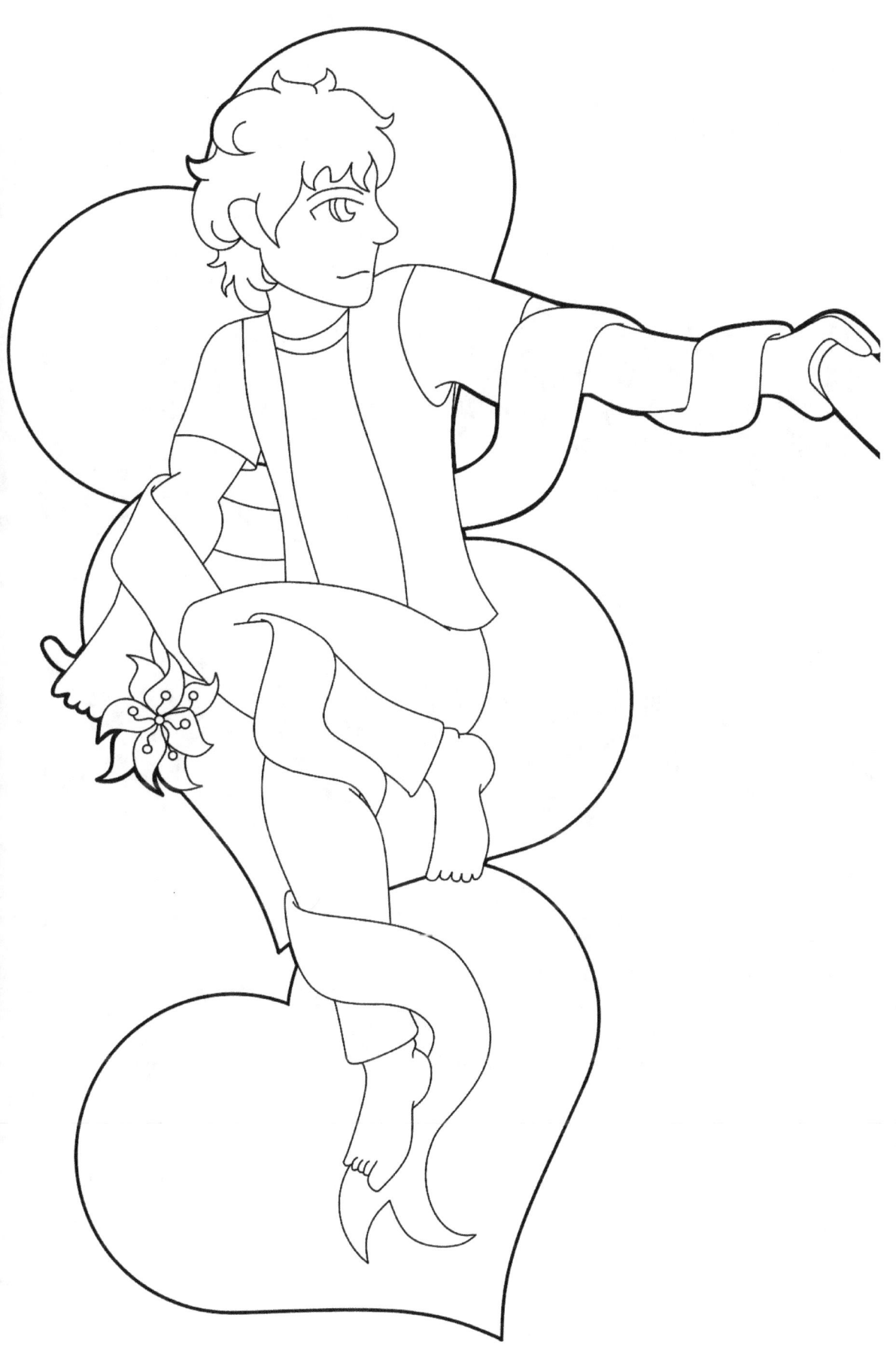

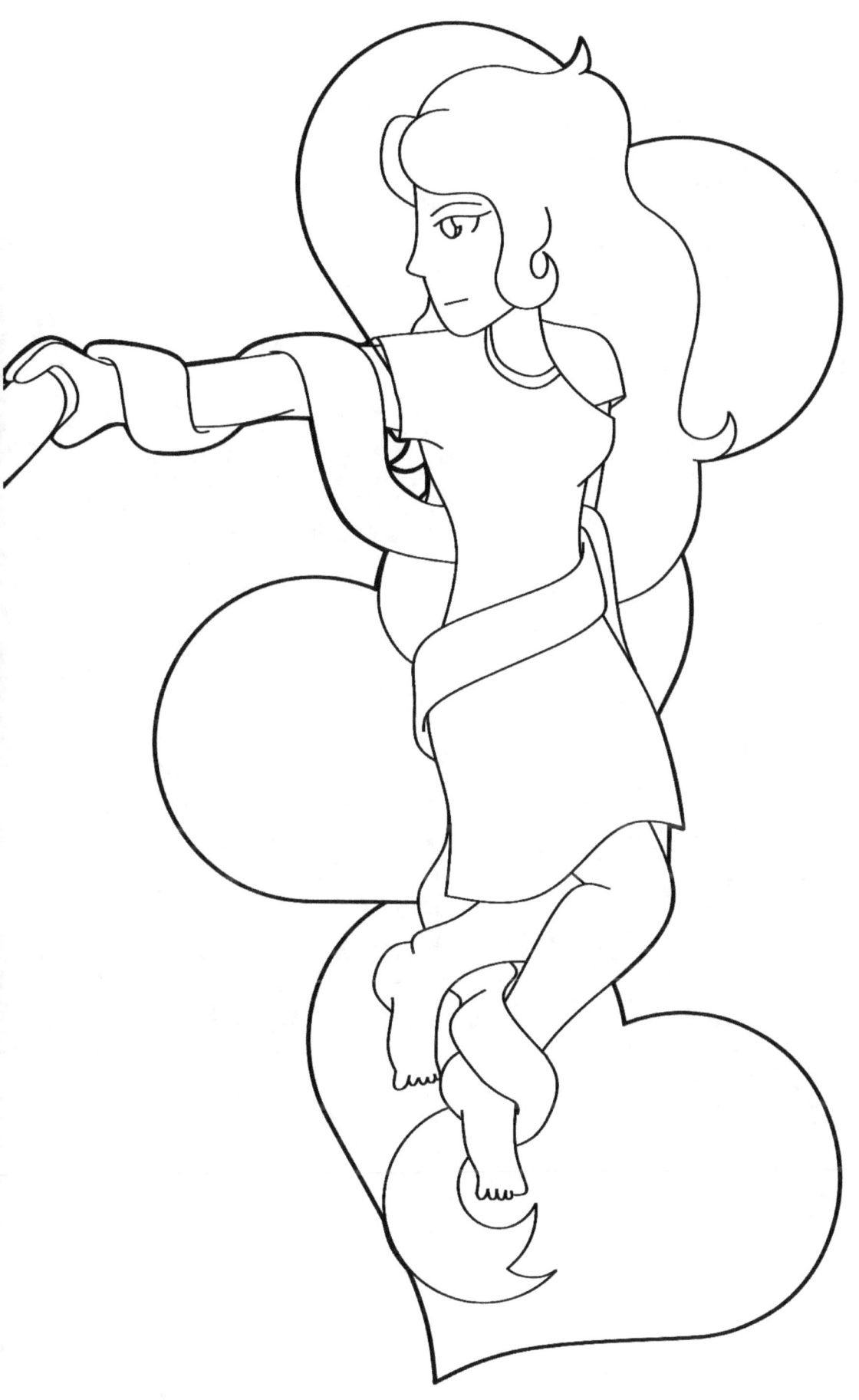

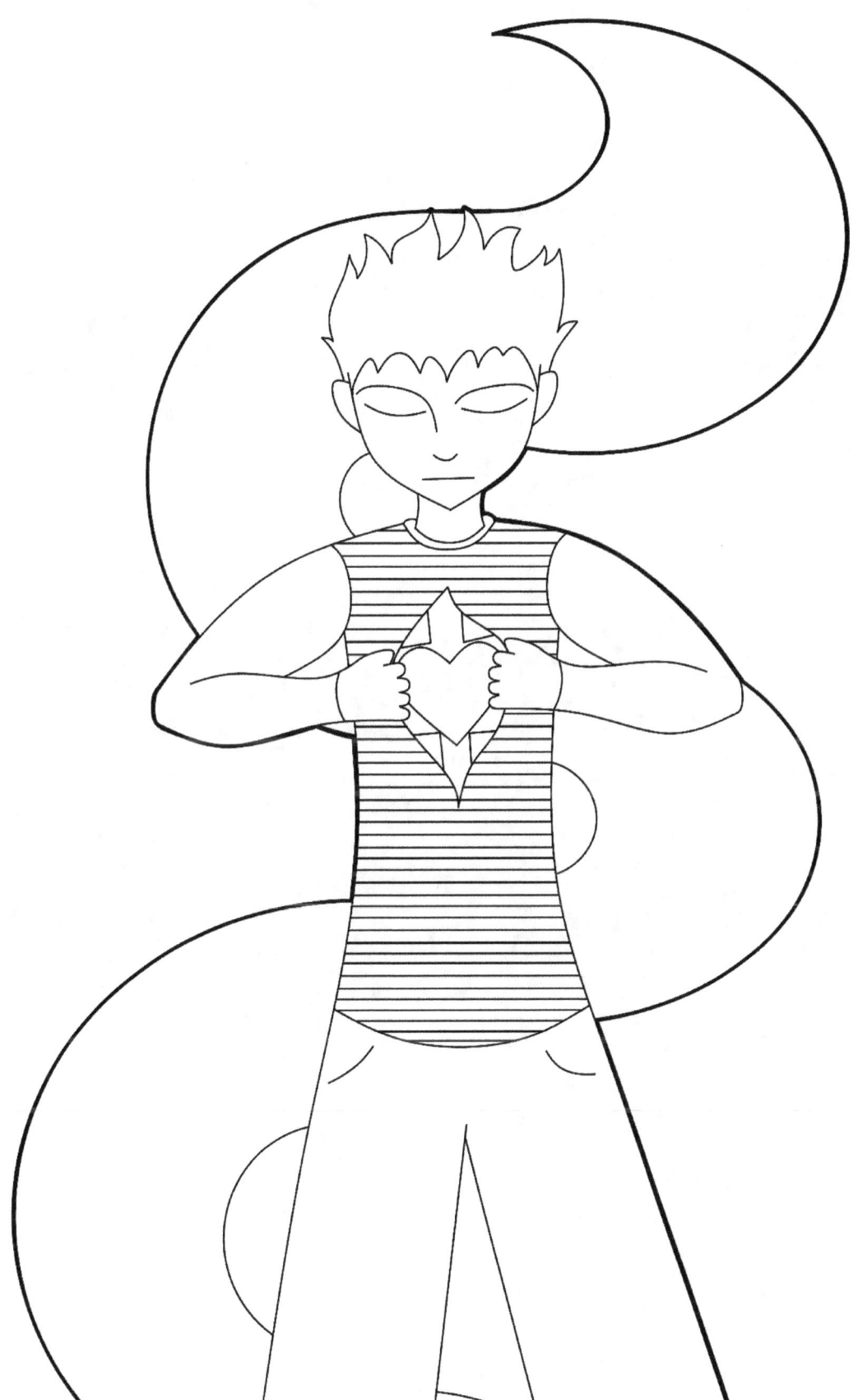

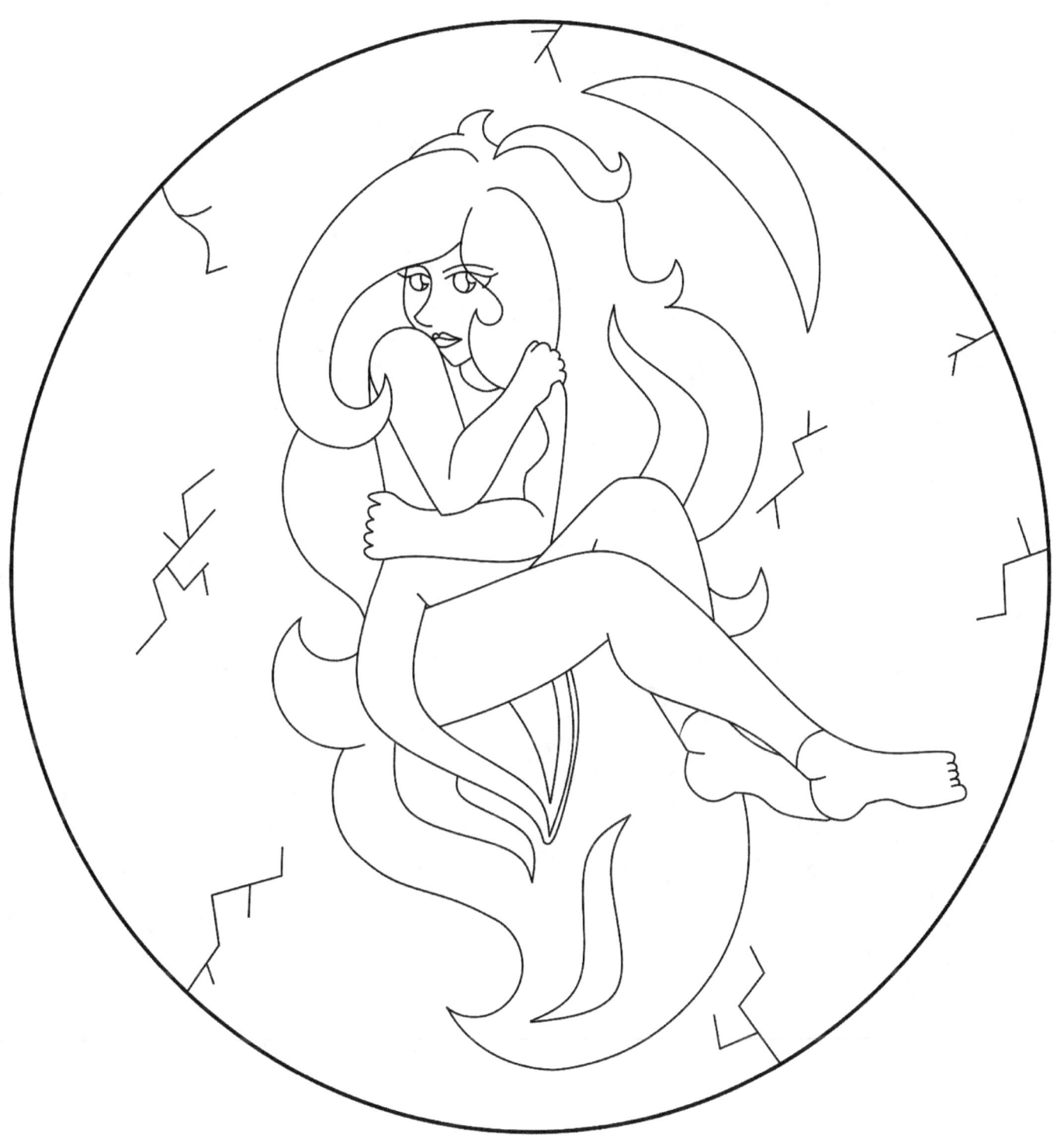

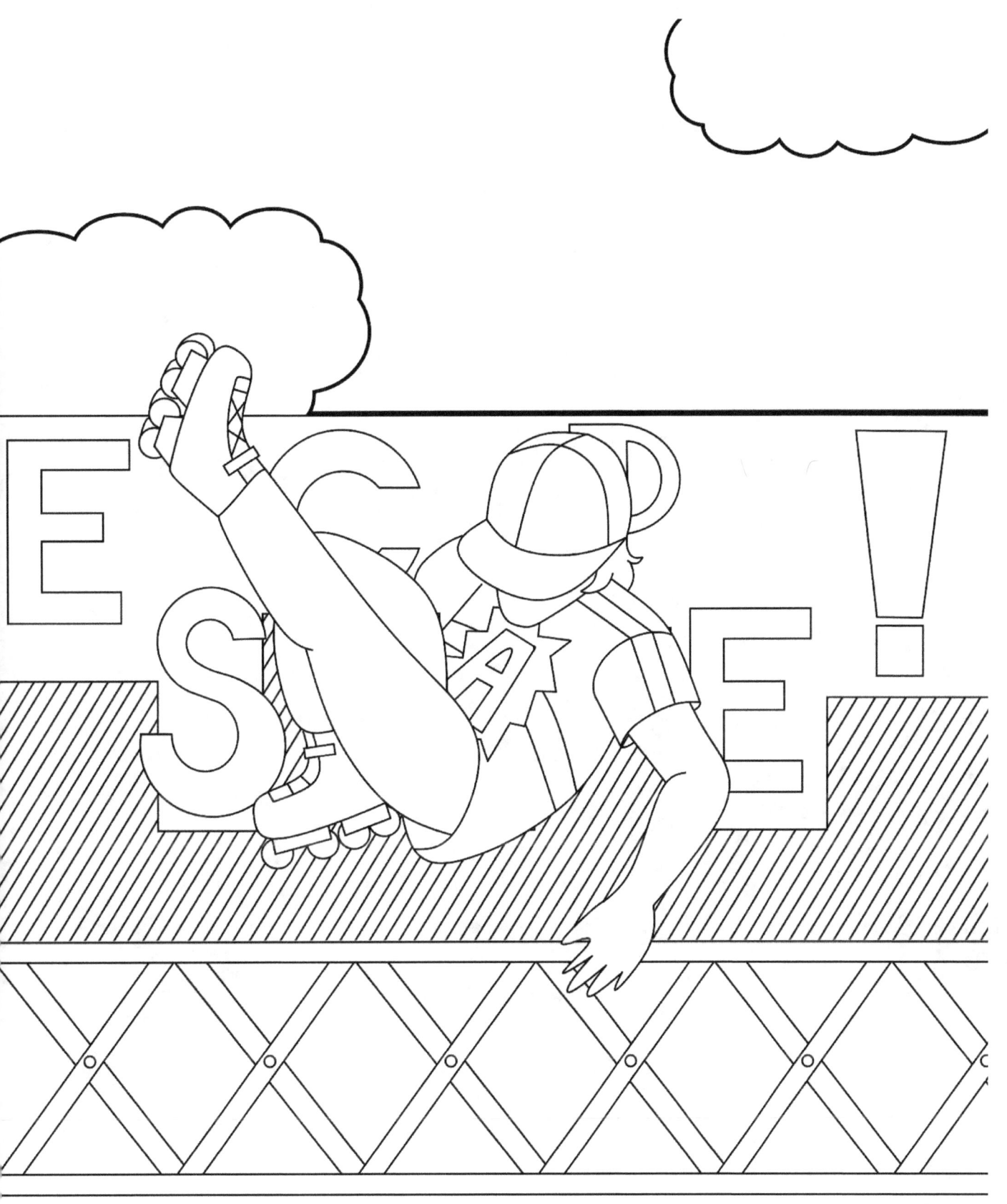

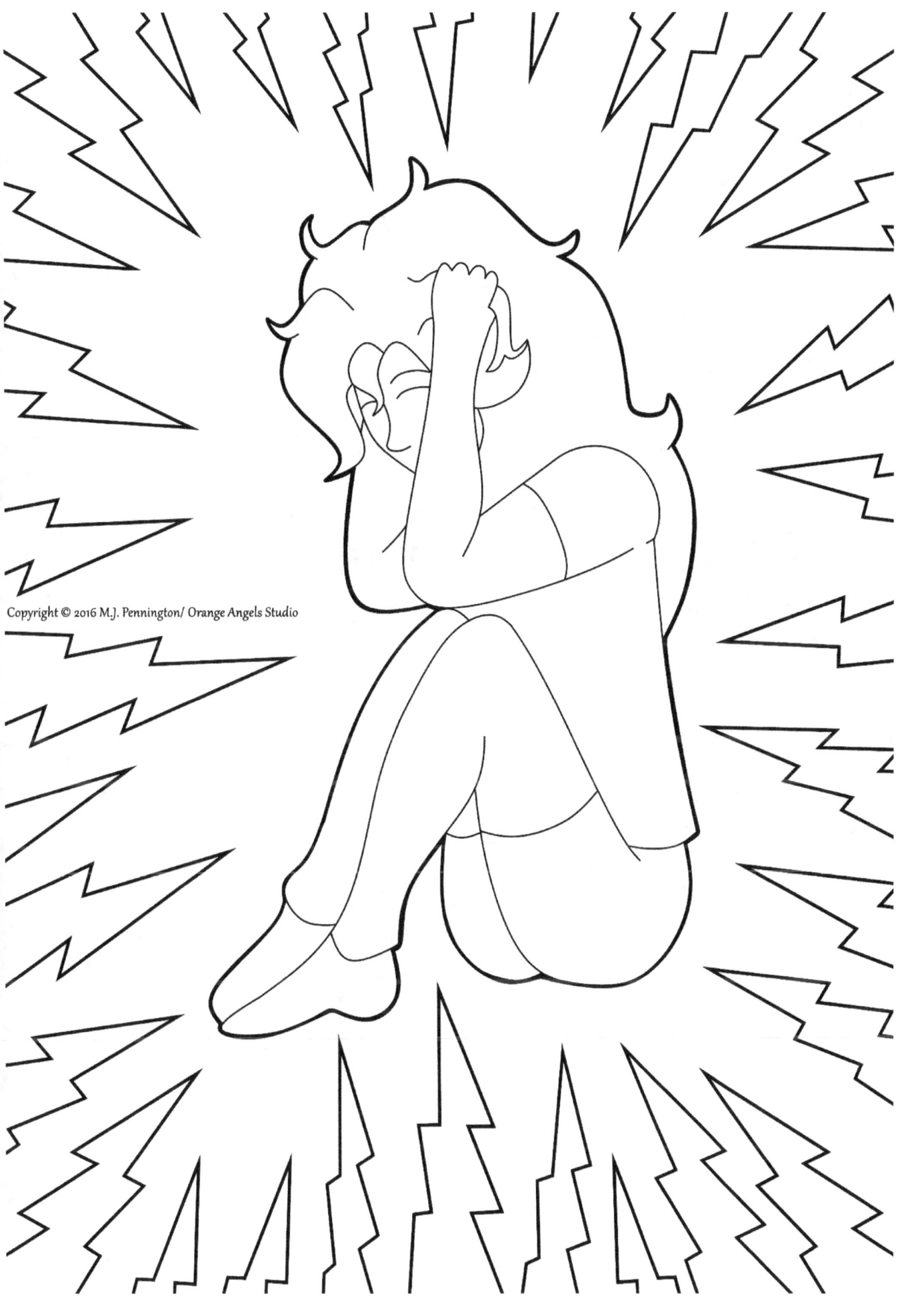

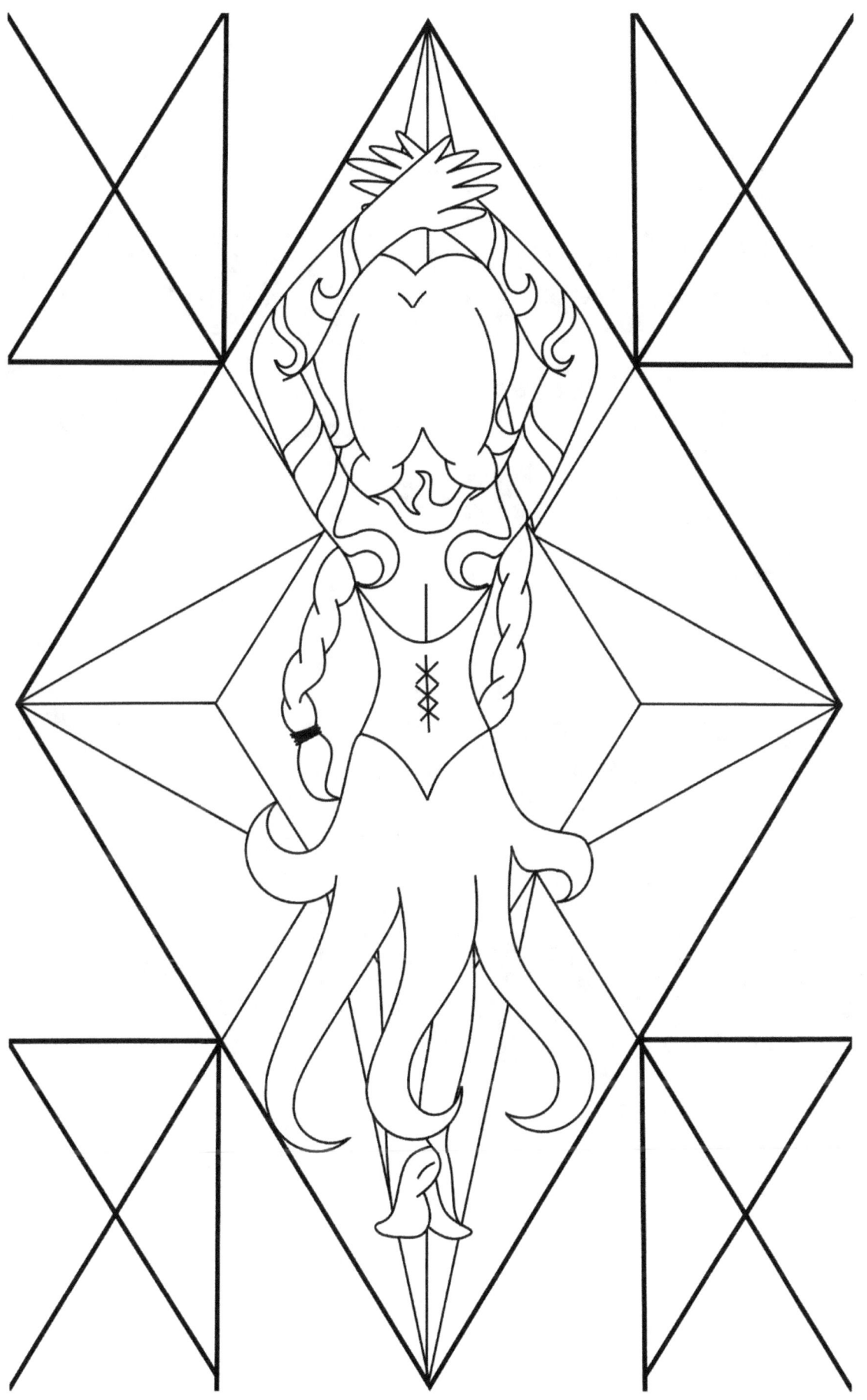

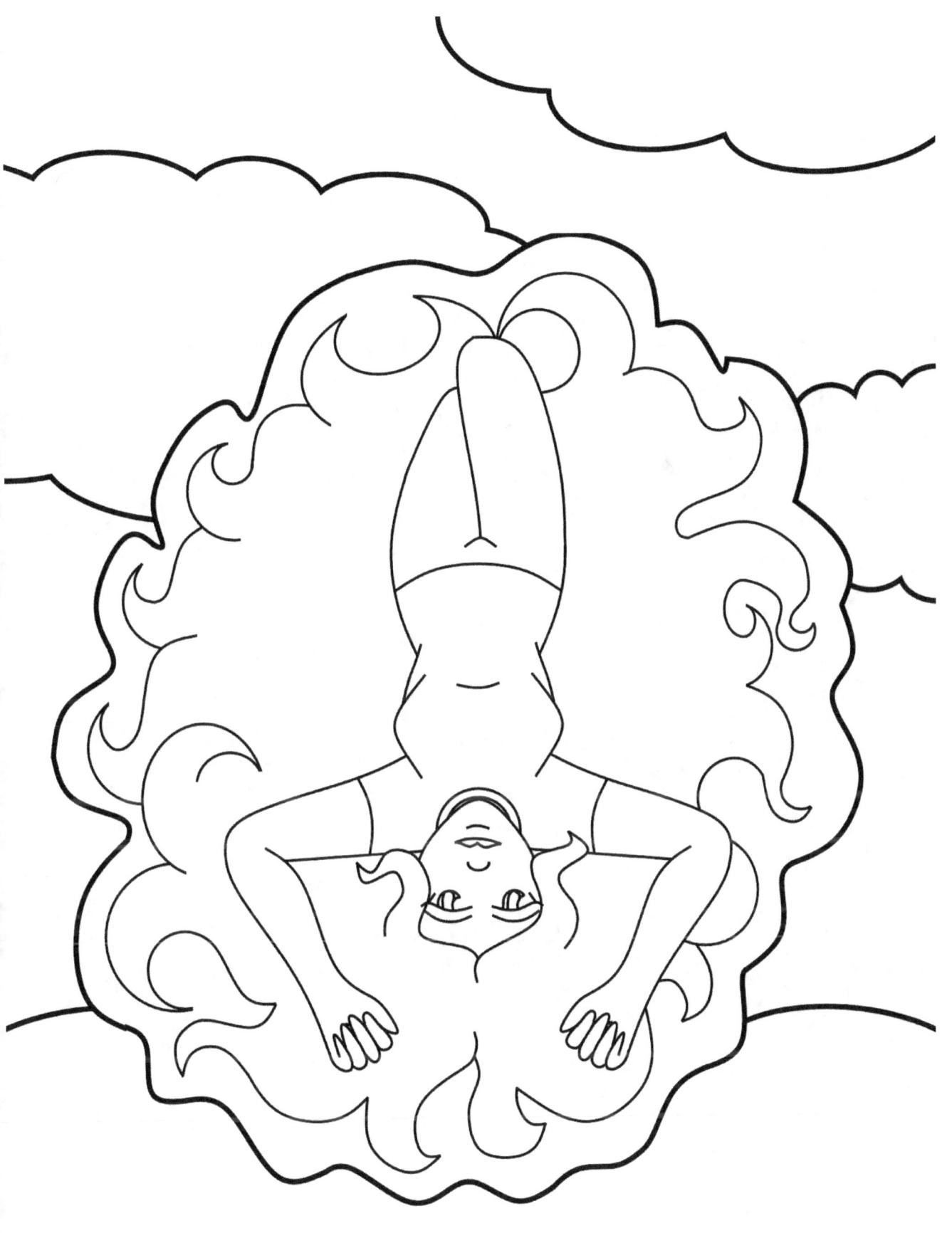

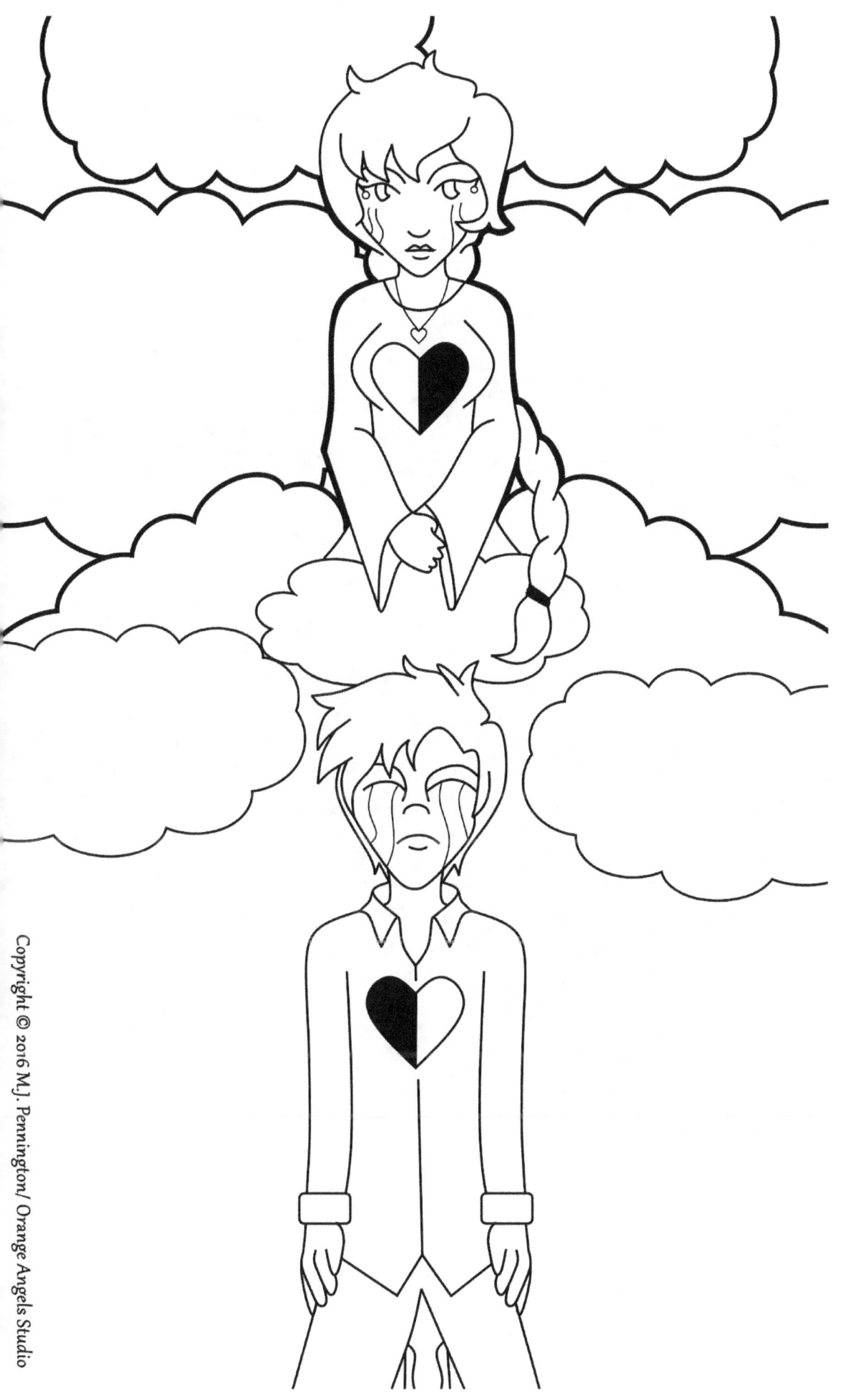

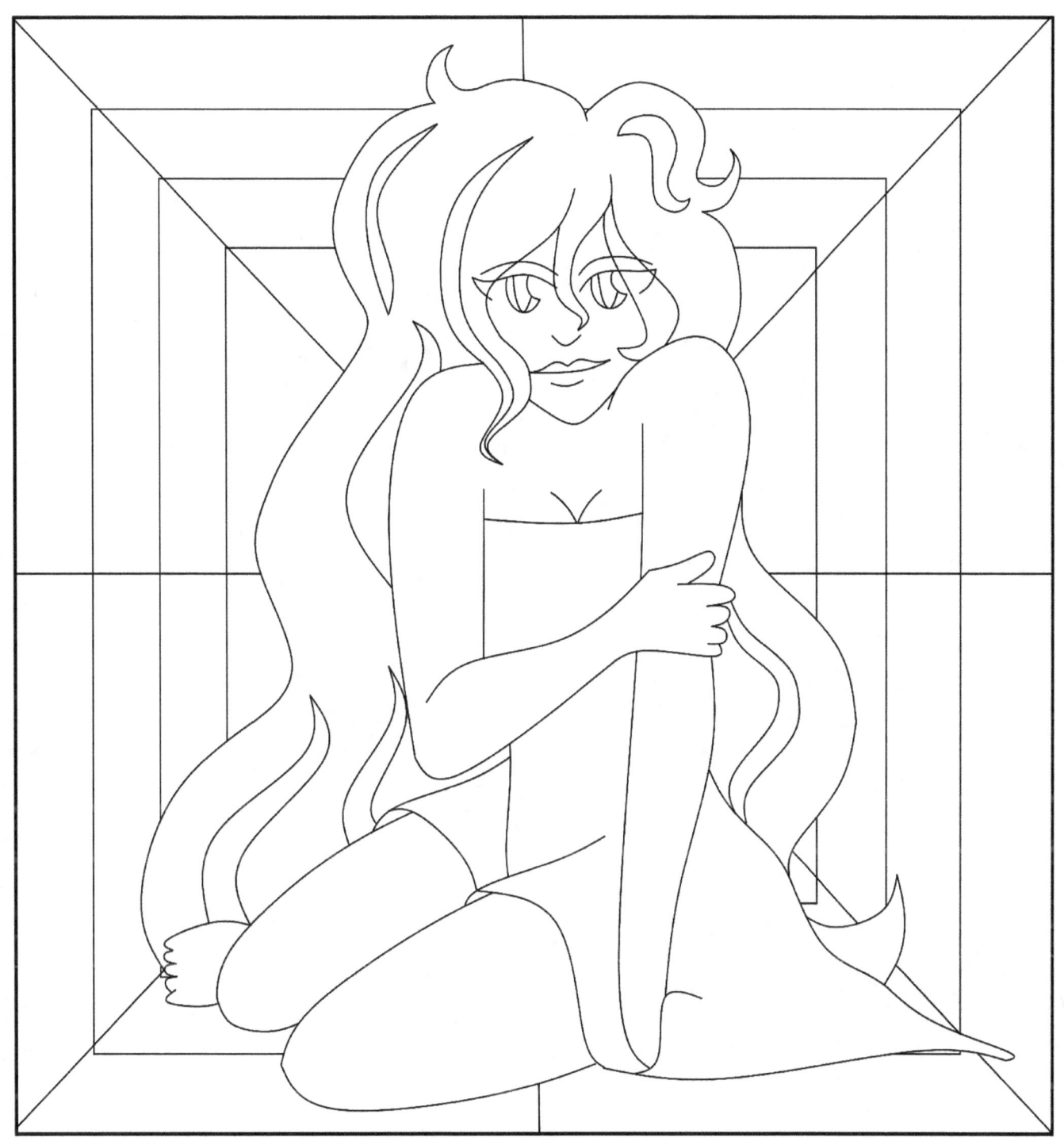

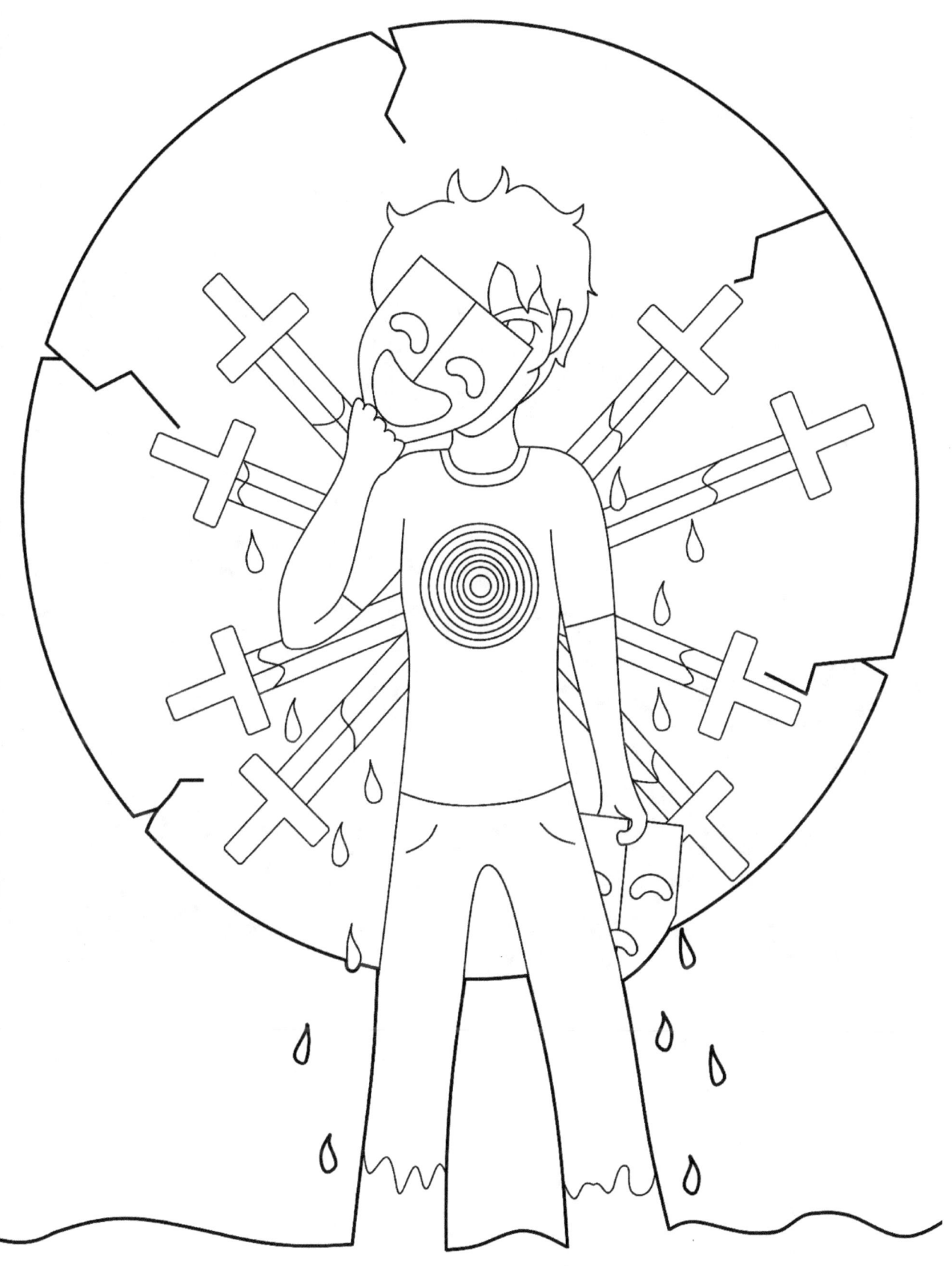

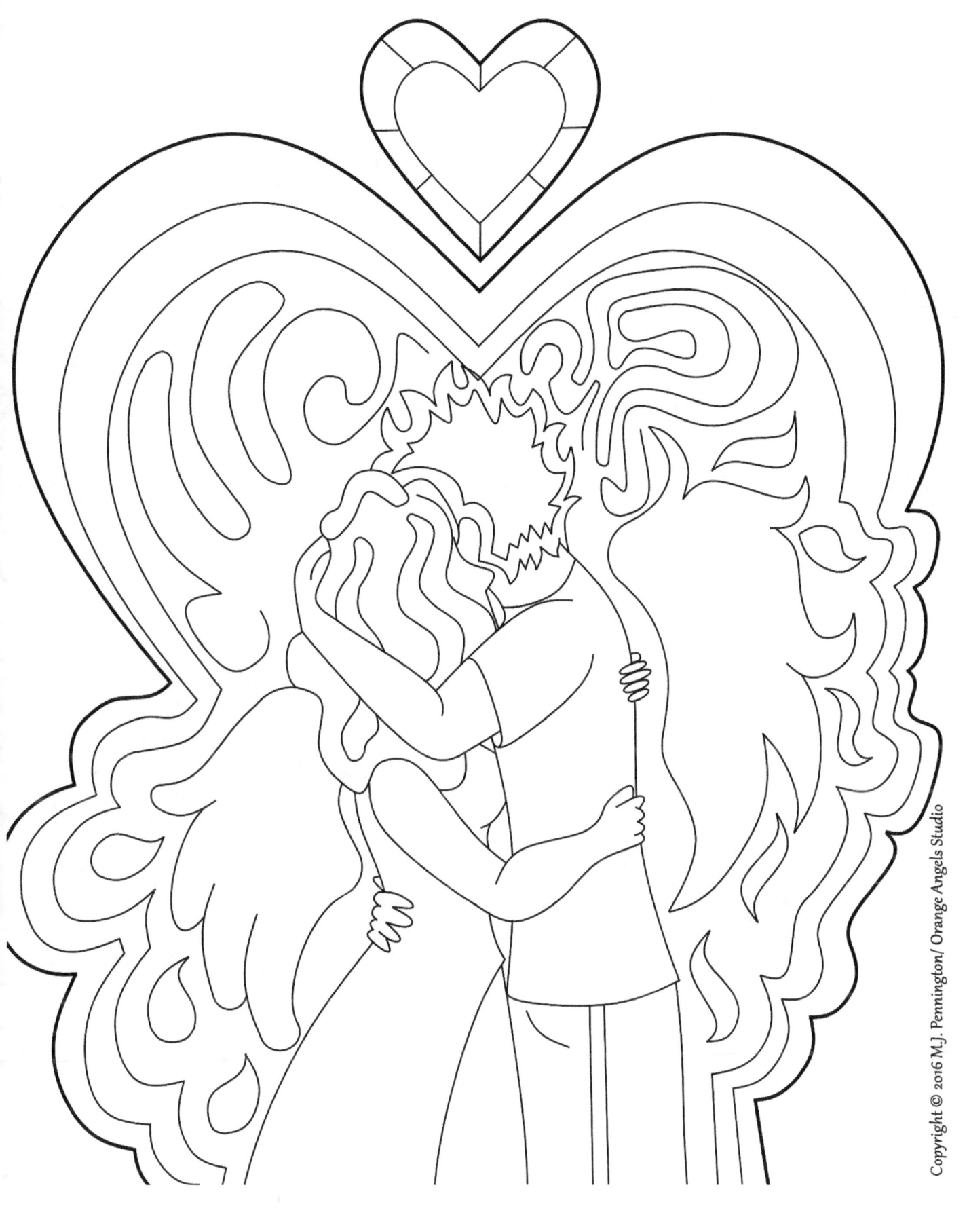

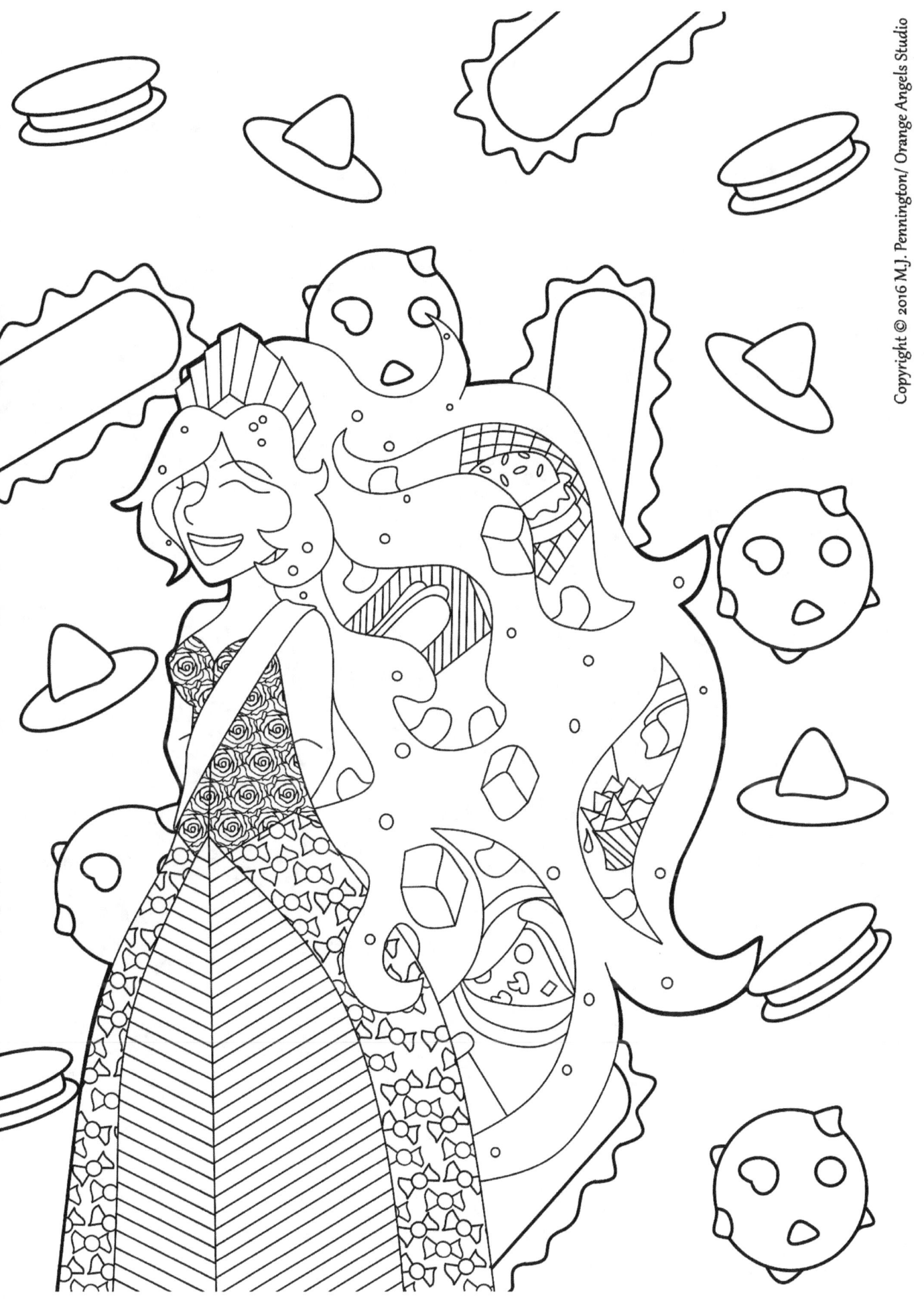

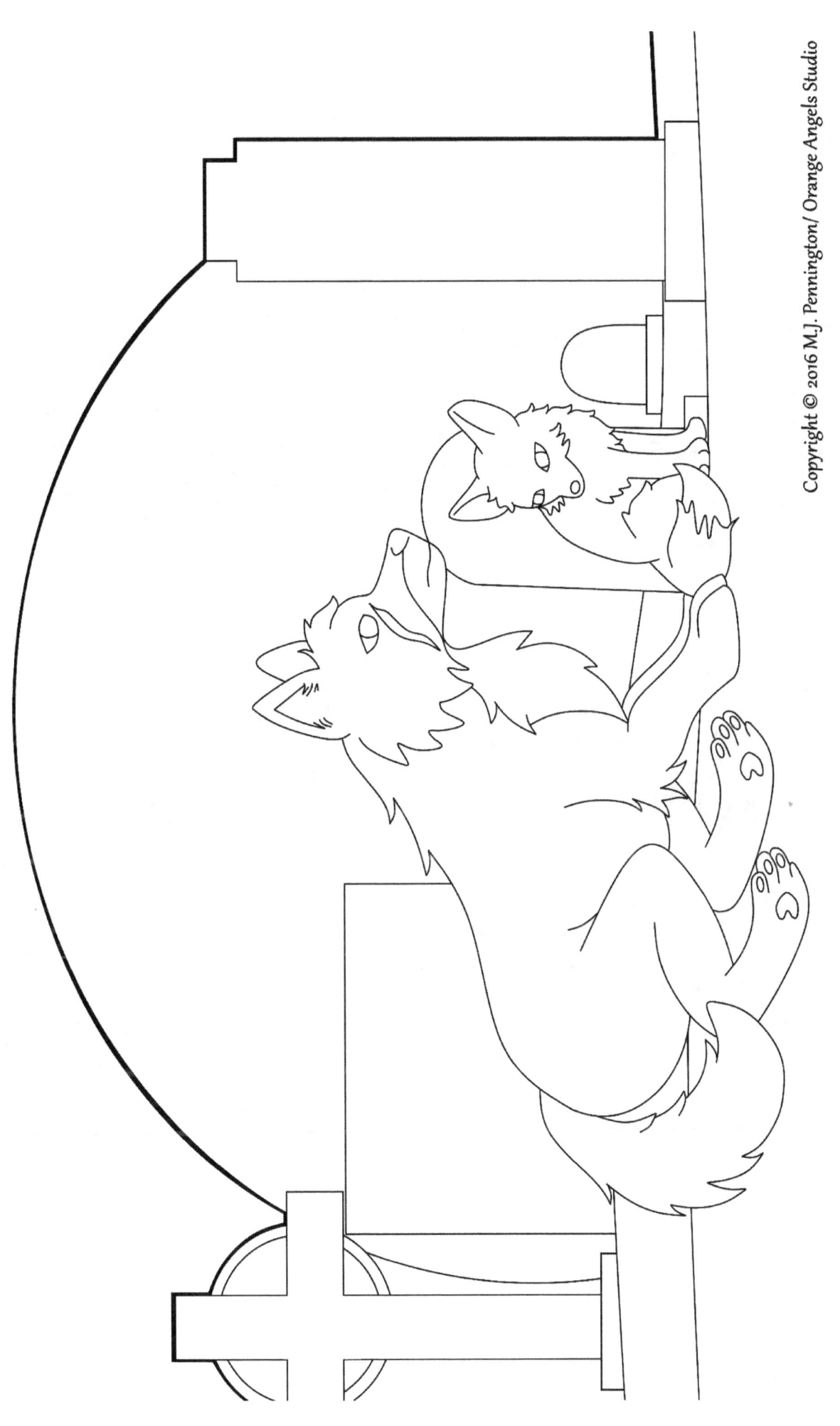

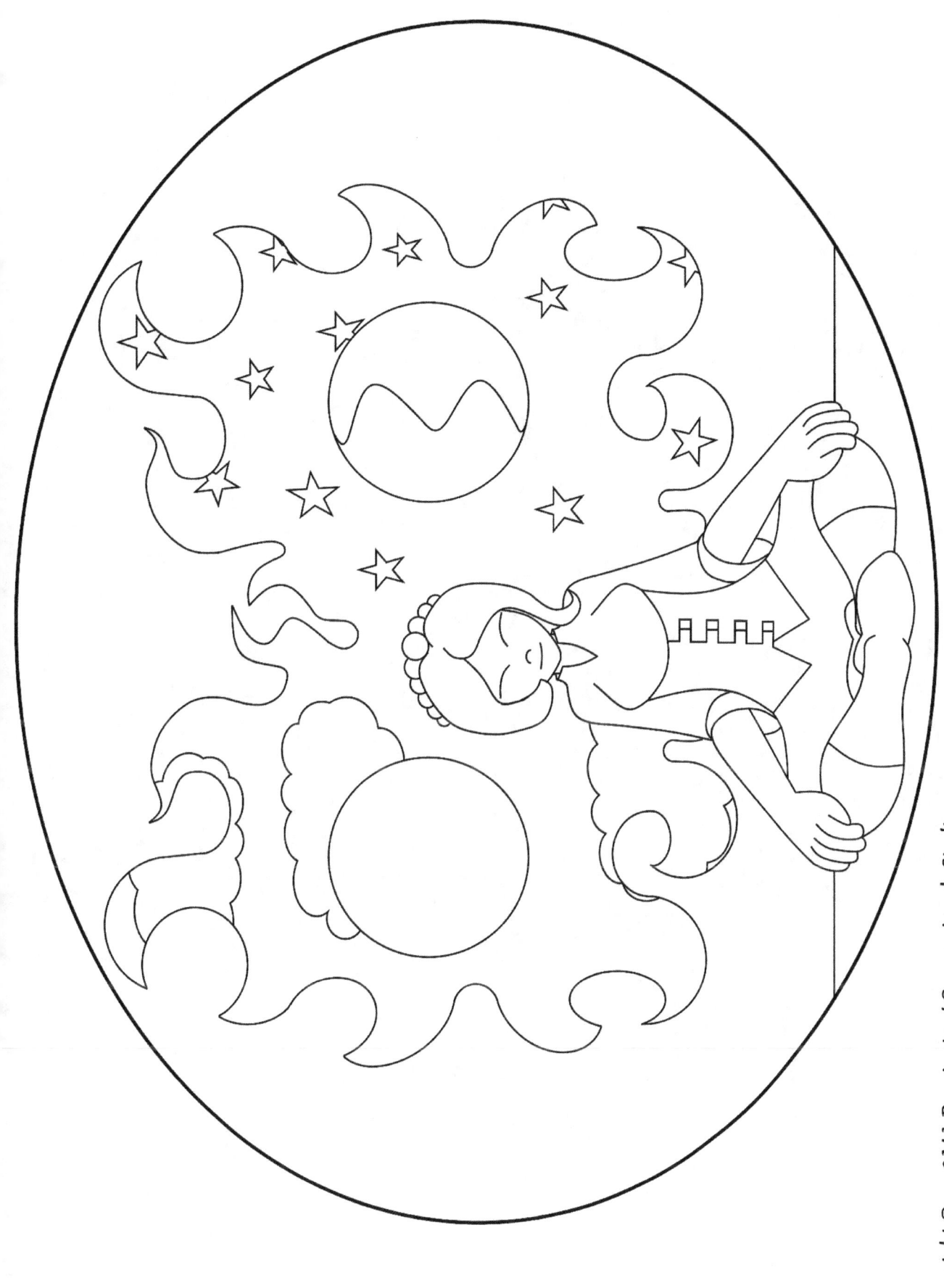

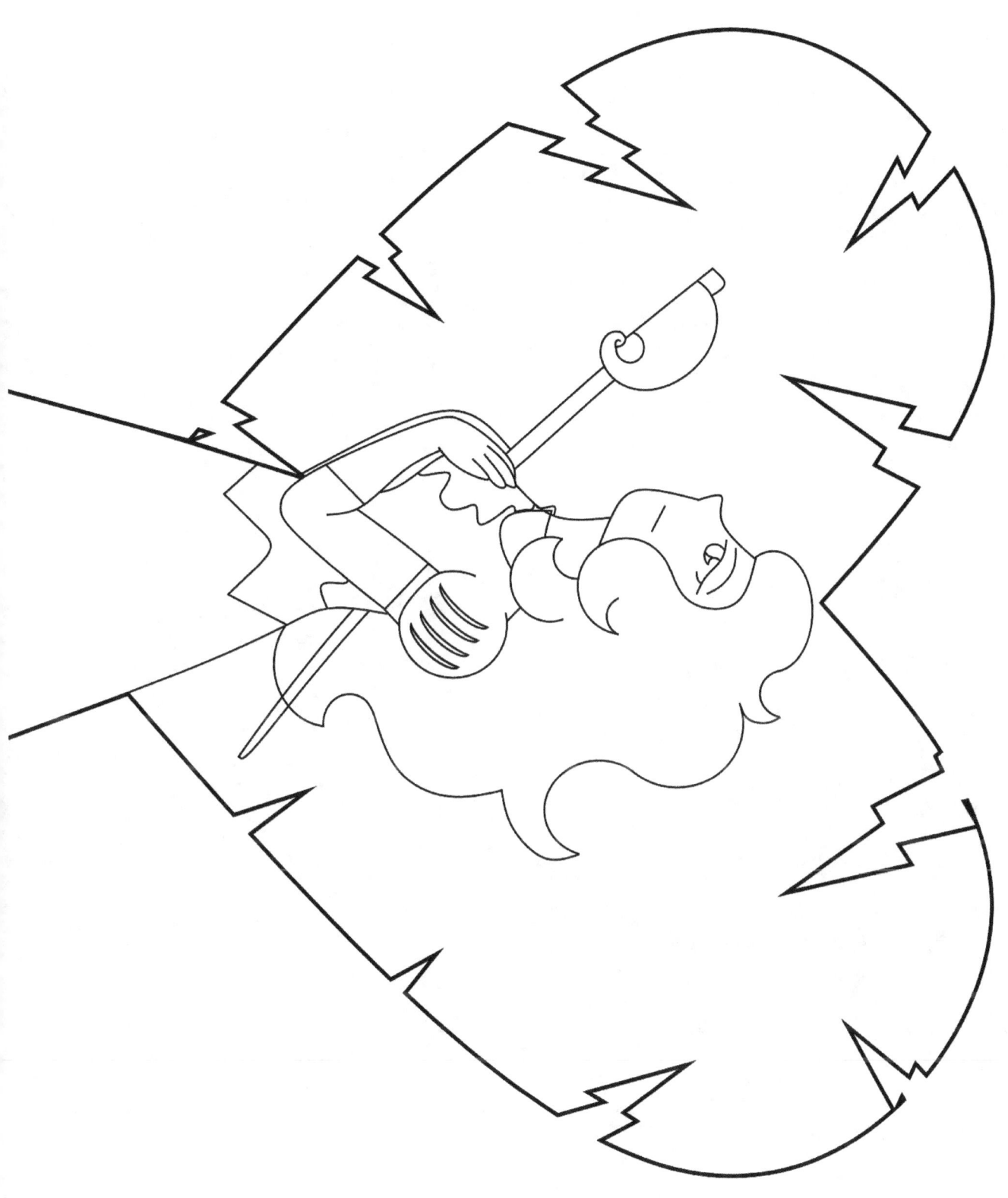

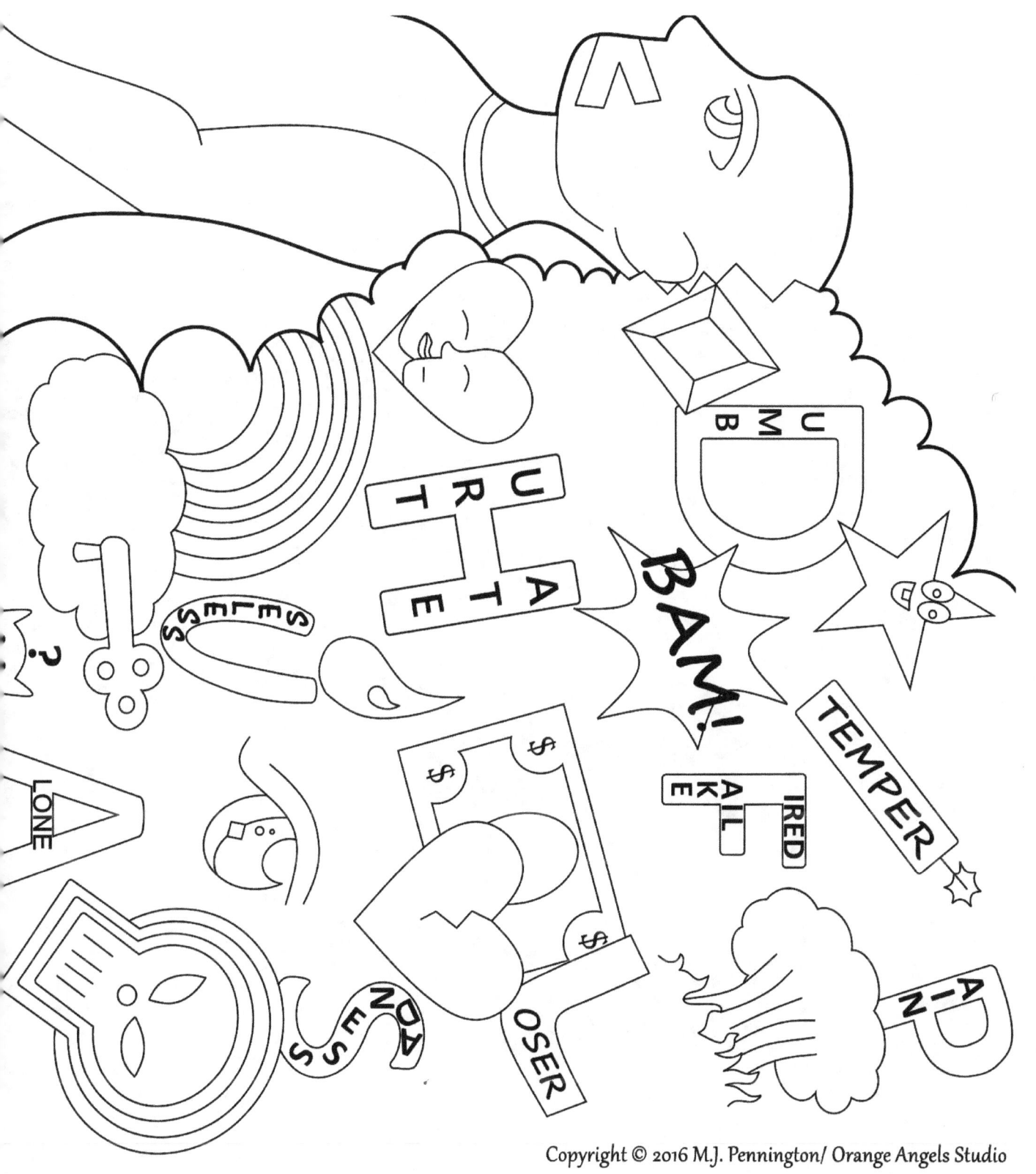

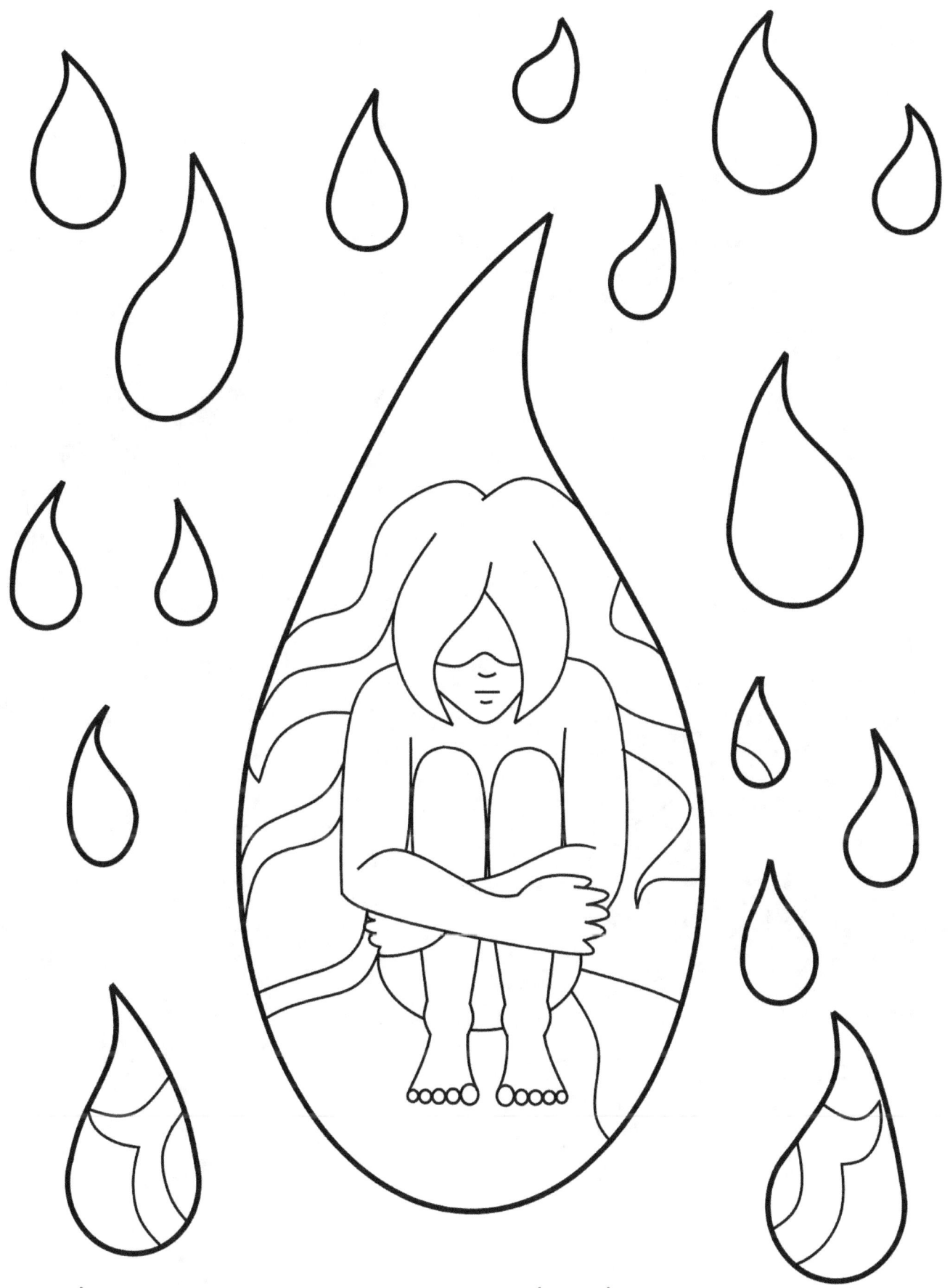

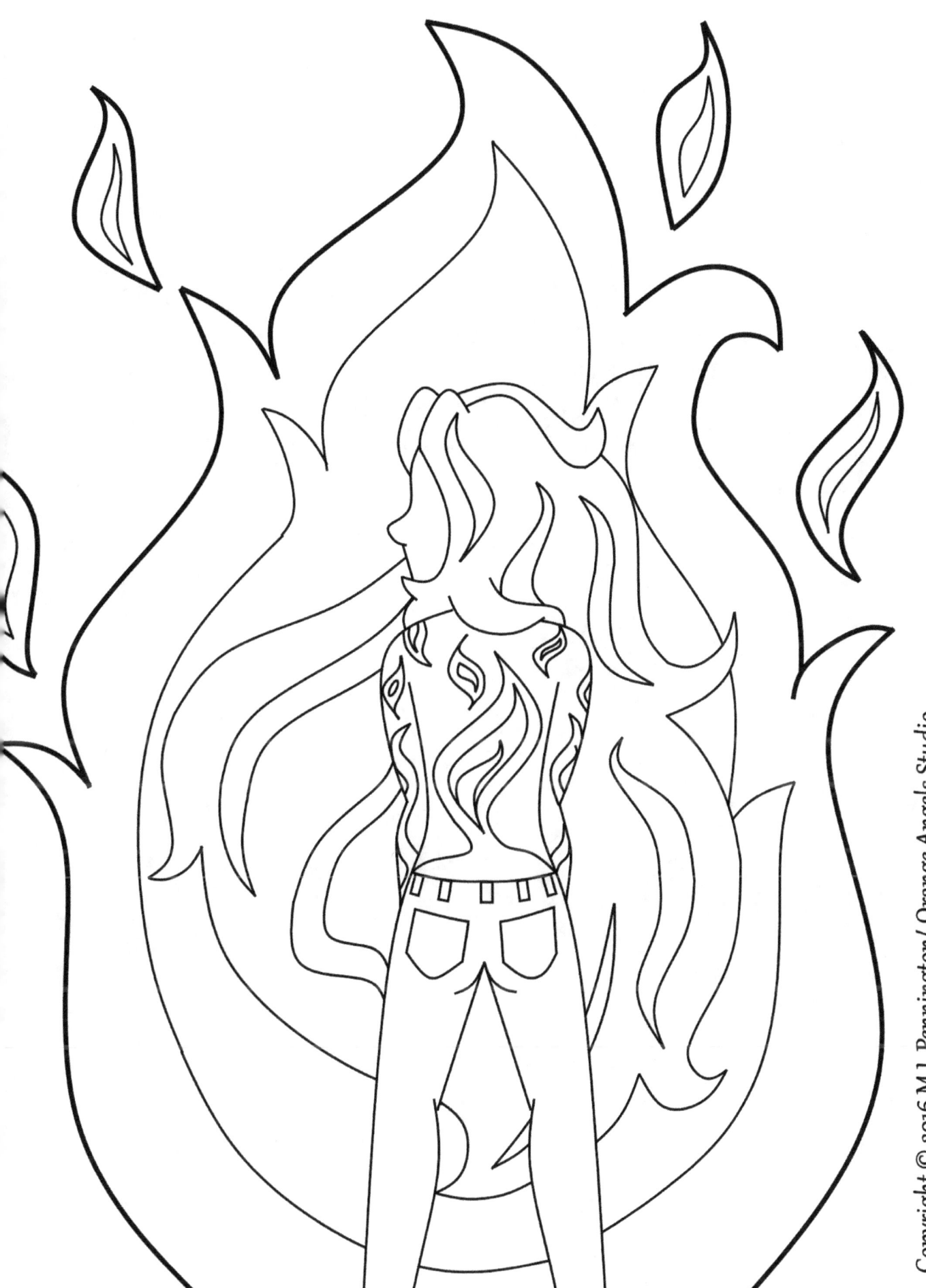

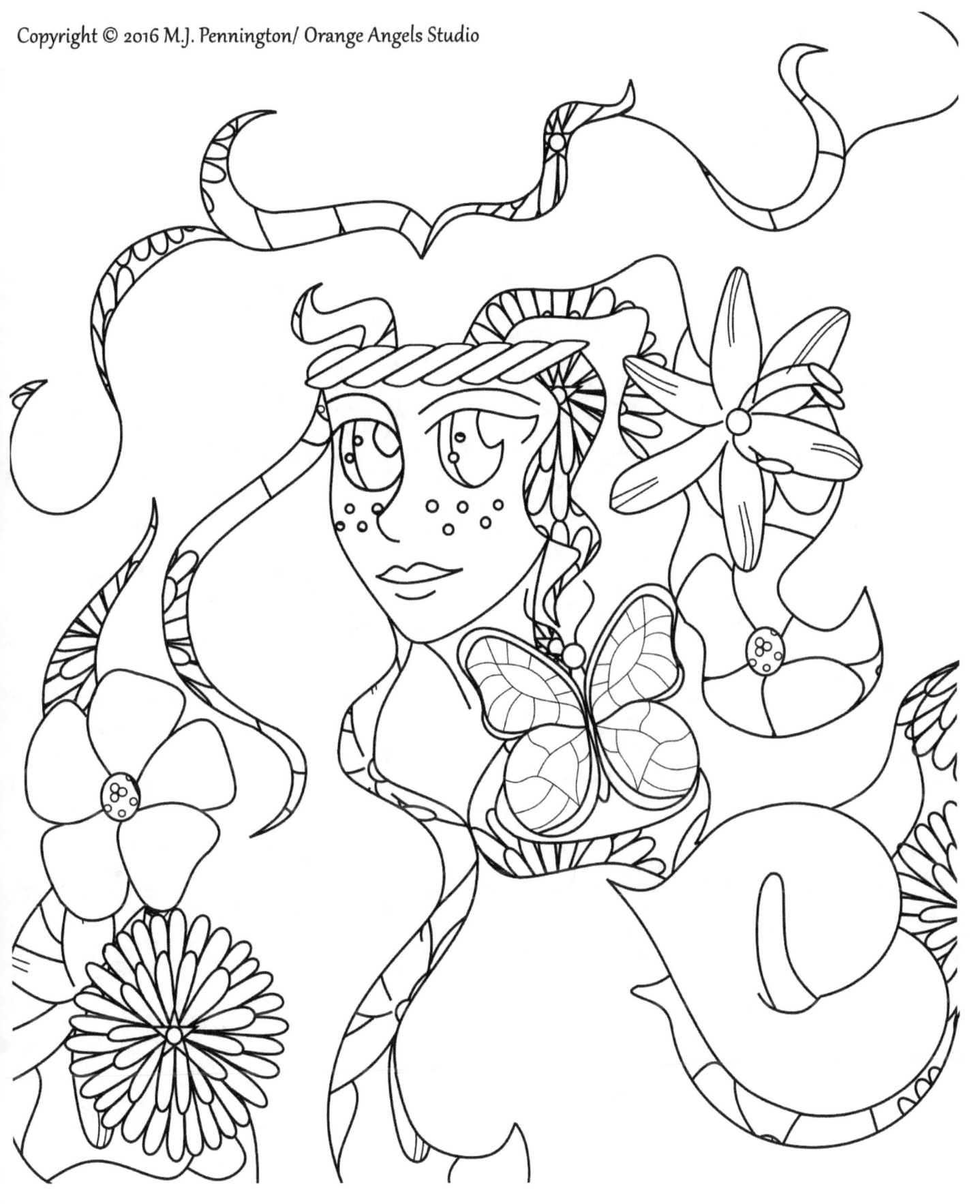

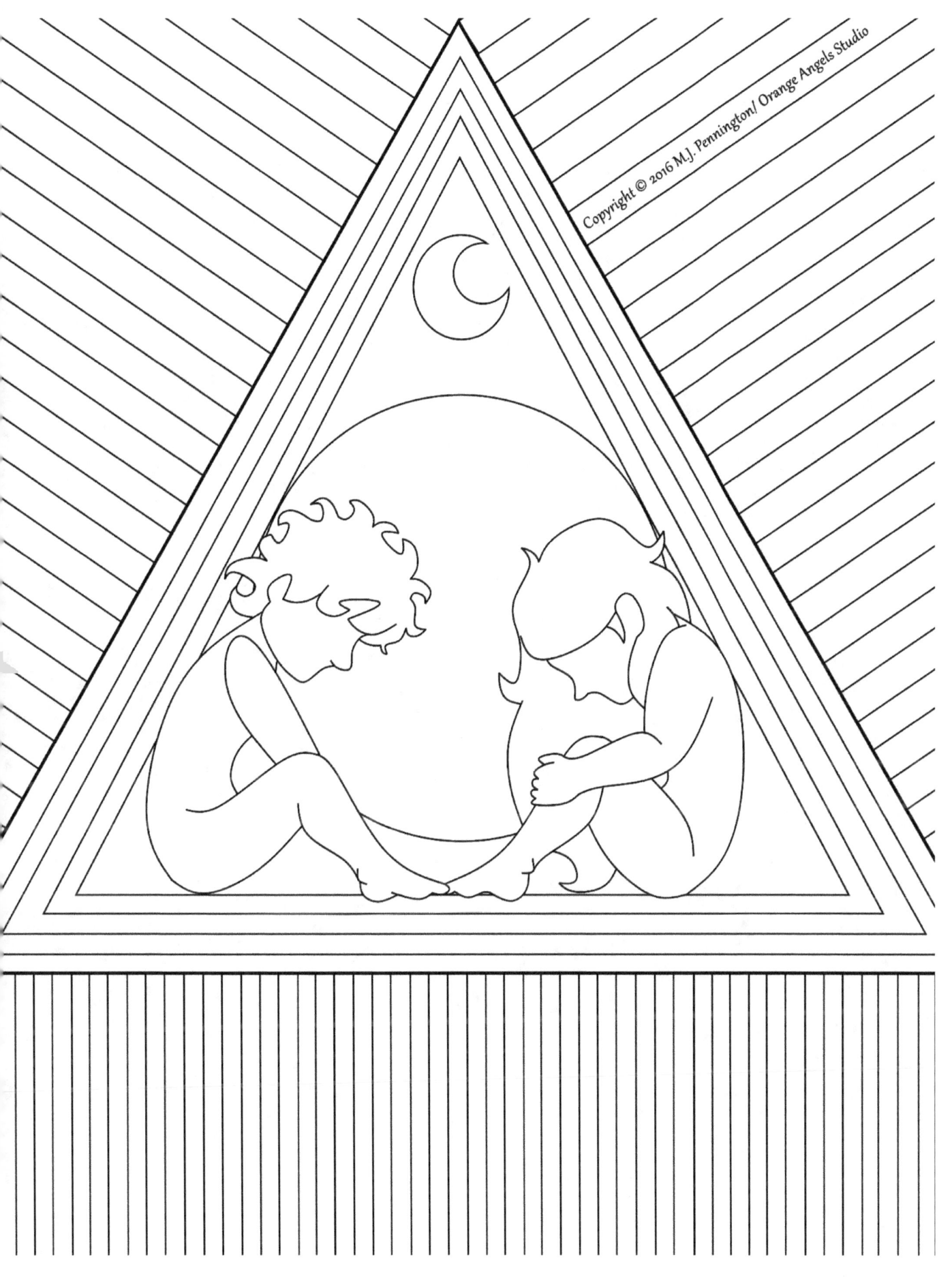

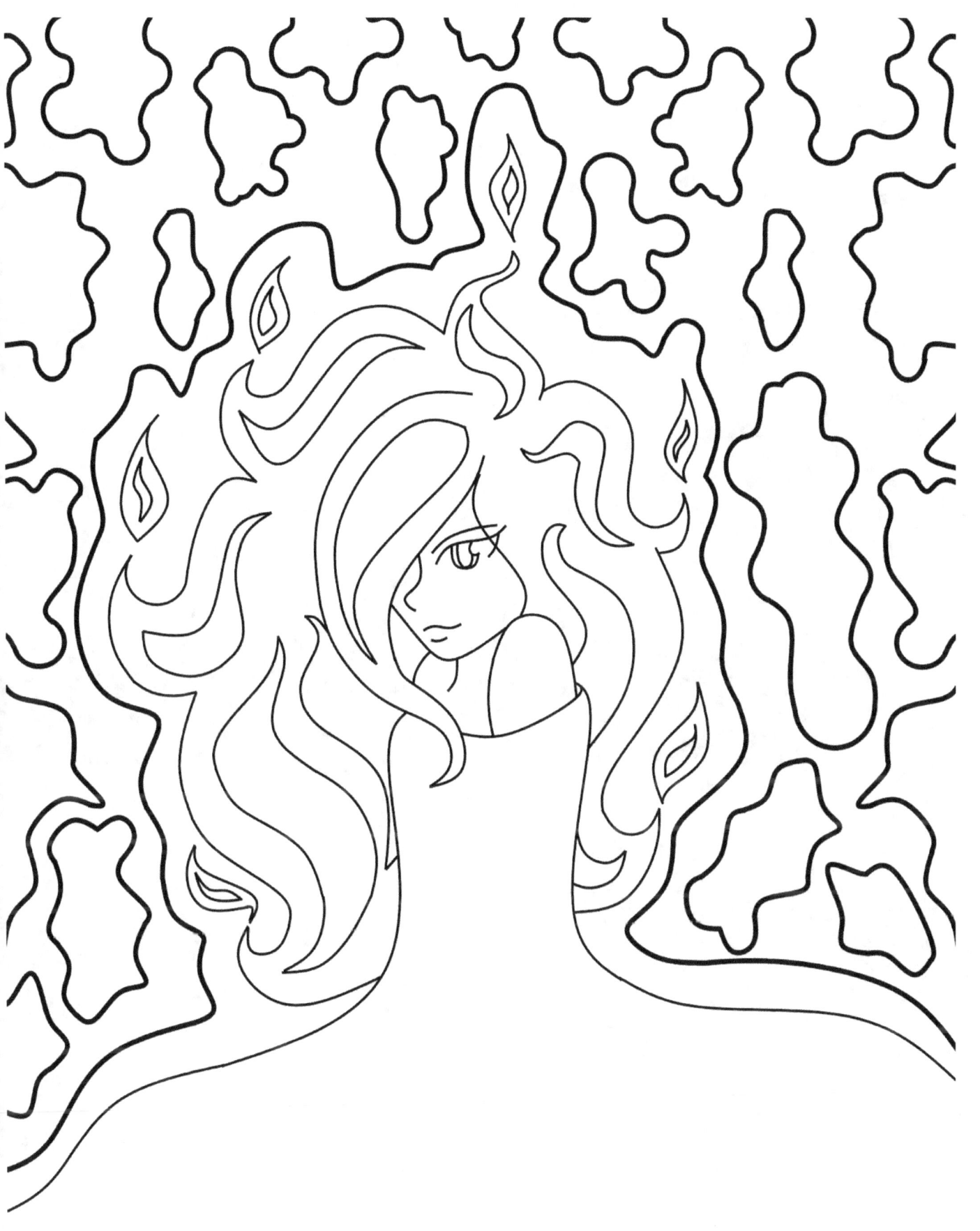

I am but a blank canvas.
Every choice I make
is a brush
stroke.

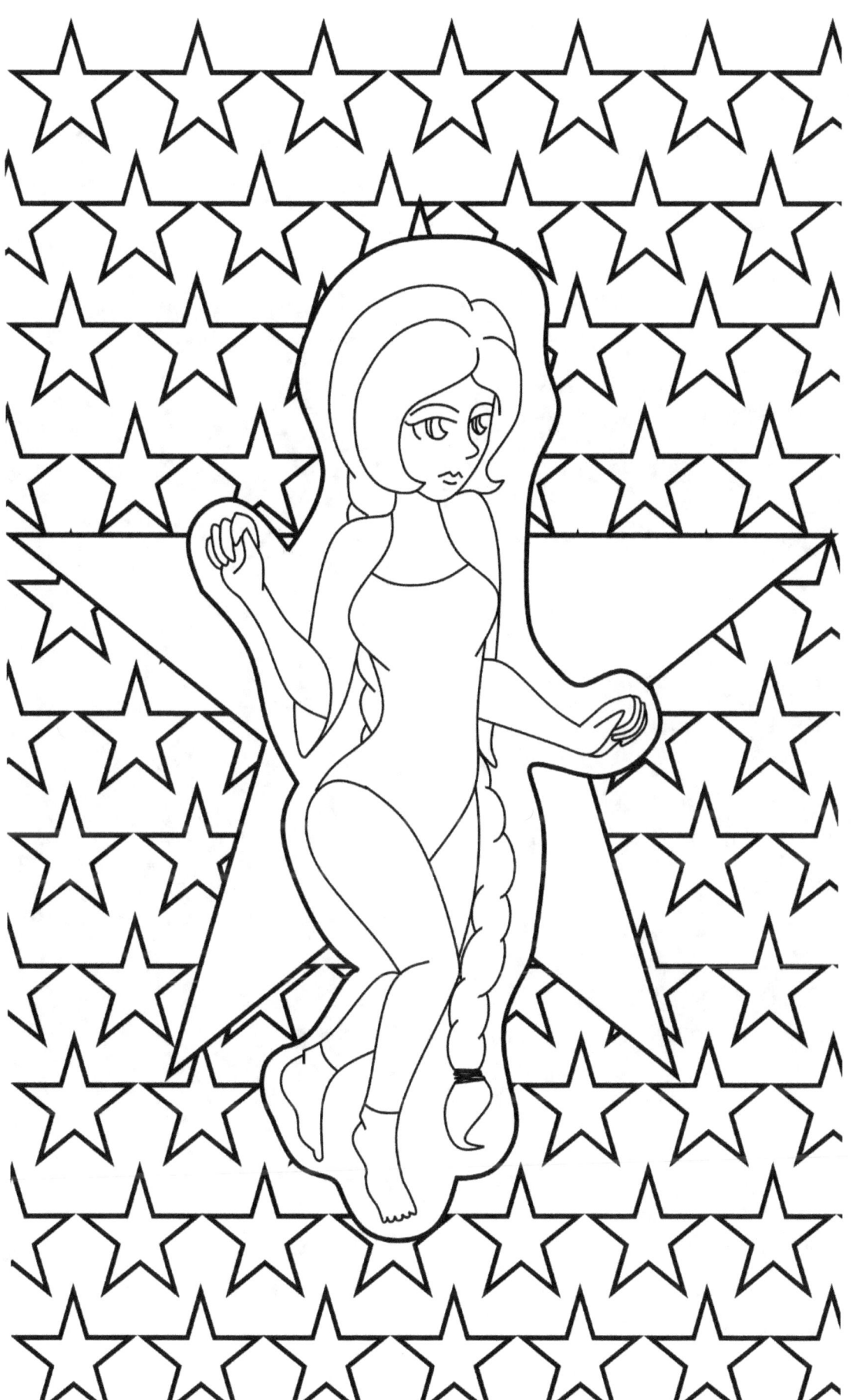

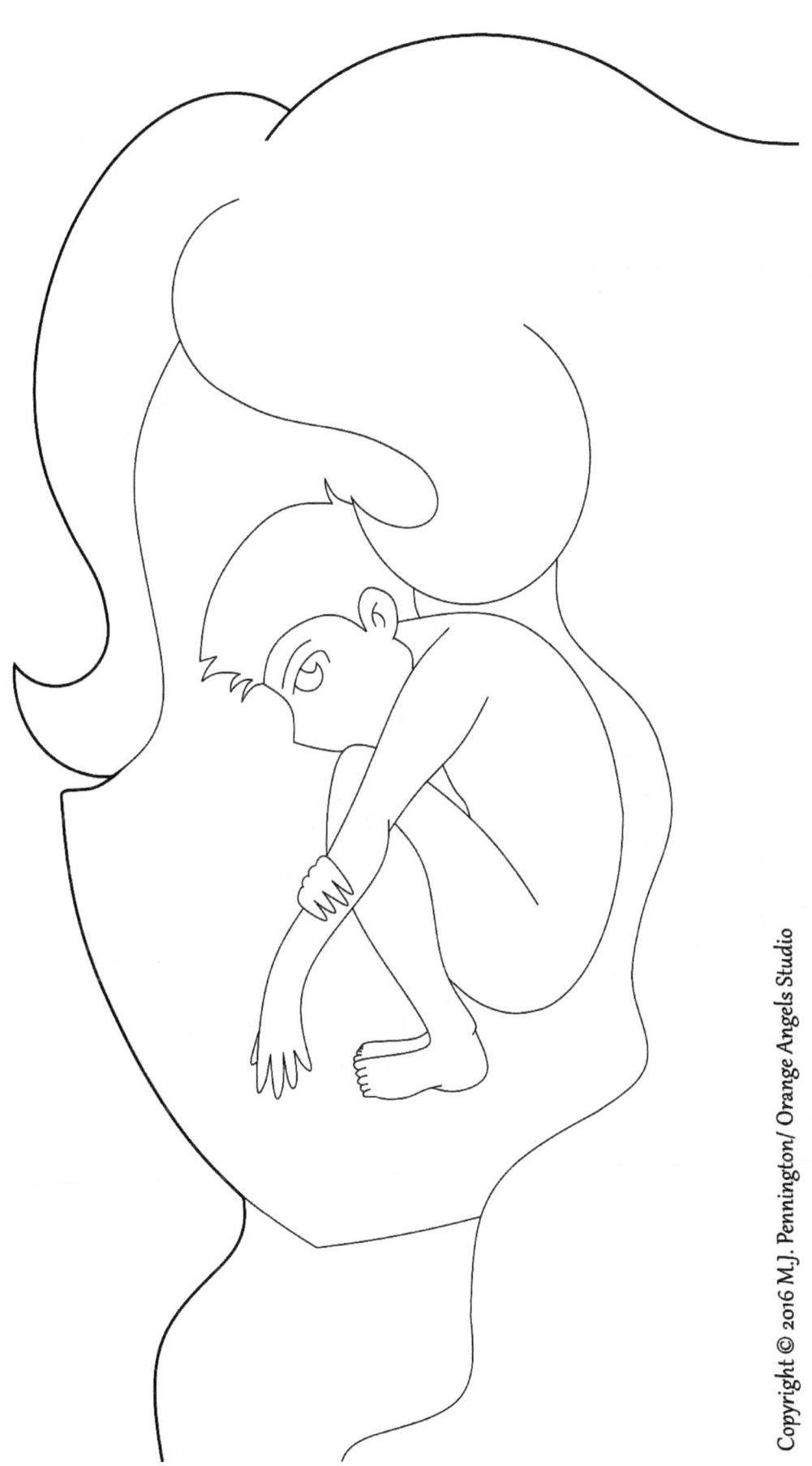

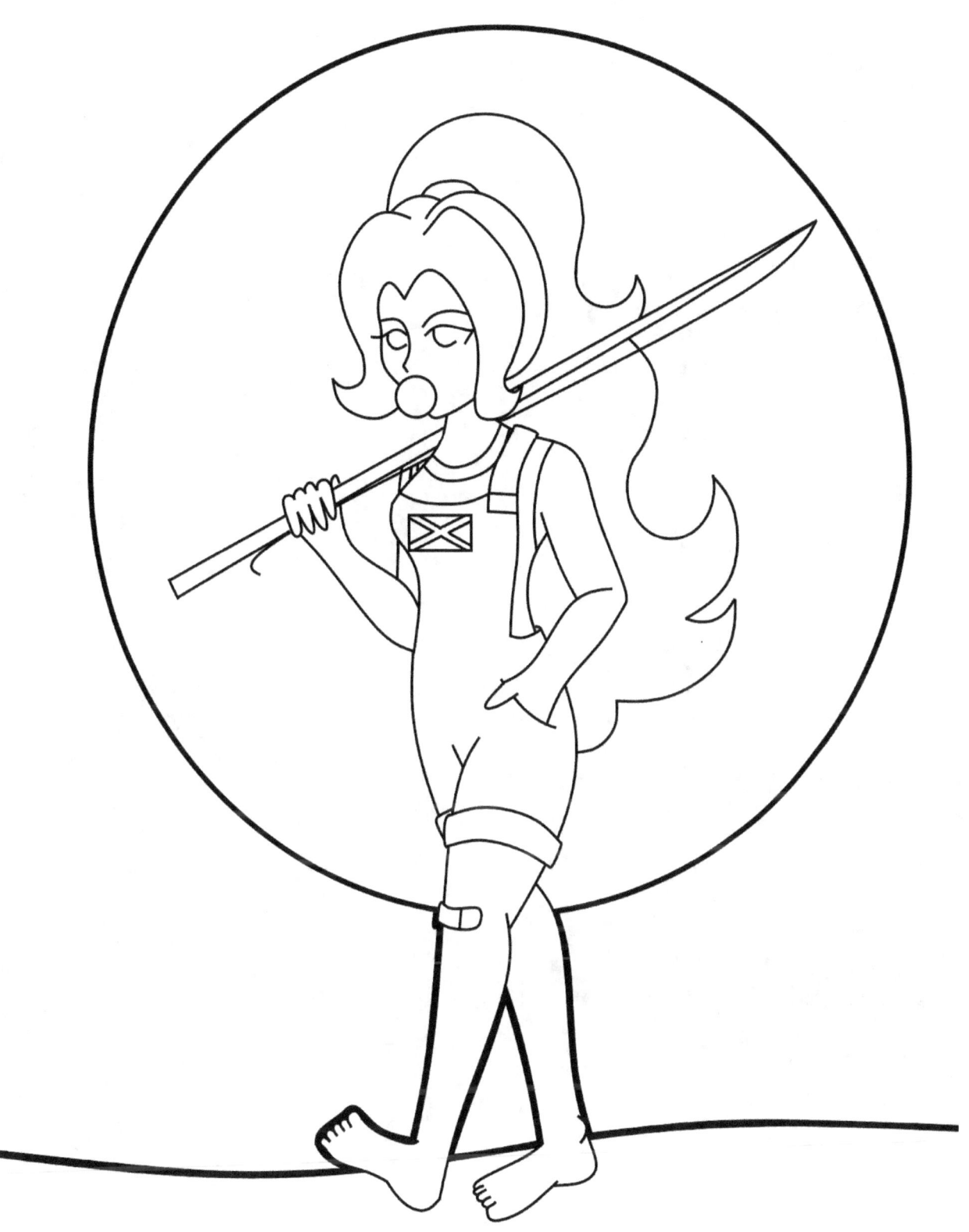

ABOUT THE ARTIST

M.J. Pennington

M.J. is a mom, artist, photographer, and cosplayer.

If you like this coloring book feel free to check out her pictures and other artwork on her studio page.

Orange Angels Studio
www.facebook.com/OrangeAngelsStudio